Altering Collective Bargaining

Charles W. Cheng

The Praeger Special Studies program—
utilizing the most modern and efficient book
production techniques and a selective
worldwide distribution network—makes
available to the academic, government, and
business communities significant, timely
research in U.S. and international economic, social, and political development.

Altering Collective Bargaining
Citizen Participation in Educational Decision Making

Praeger Publishers   New York   Washington   London

PRAEGER SPECIAL STUDIES IN U.S. ECONOMIC, SOCIAL, AND POLITICAL ISSUES

Library of Congress Cataloging in Publication Data

Cheng, Charles W
    Altering collective bargaining.

    (Praeger special studies in U.S. economics, social, and political issues)
    Bibliography: p.
    Includes index.
    1. Collective bargaining—Teachers—United States.
I. Title.
LB2842.2.C53   331.89'041'371100973   75-36415
ISBN 0-275-56300-6

PRAEGER PUBLISHERS
111 Fourth Avenue, New York, N.Y. 10003, U.S.A.

Published in the United States of America in 1976
by Praeger Publishers, Inc.

ACKNOWLEDGMENTS

This study stems from my active participation in the teachers
union movement in 1961-72. I owe a great deal to the rank-and-file
members of the Washington Teachers Union and also to my close
friend David Elsila, editor of <u>American Teacher</u>, who sparked me
to think more deeply about the implications teacher bargaining might
hold for other groups that are excluded from the negotiating process.

This study would not have been possible without the assistance
and encouragement of many people. A number of people at Harvard
University were particularly helpful. My colleague and friend Ron
Edmonds has helped immensely by providing resources for its final-
writing stages. Frank Duehay has played an important role over the
last three years in helping me formulate and organize the plans for
this work. Joseph Featherstone's teachings, comments, and insights
have helped to sharpen the focus of this work. Kenneth Haskin's comments on the original draft have been invaluable, and his uninhibited
criticism has greatly improved the quality of this study. Further,
his own work and his daily commitment to the Black Liberation struggle have been a source of strength and inspiration.

I am profoundly indebted to my colleague and friend William
Greenbaum, who took enormous time from his own busy schedule to
offer critical commentary. I would also like to thank another colleague
and friend, Marsha Hirano, for carefully proofreading the final manu-
script. Bonny Ogent and Ann Smith did an excellent job in the typing.
I also wish to thank Don Davies and the Institute for Responsive Education at Boston University for providing me with the necessary resources to conduct the field research. Finally, my wife Judy has my
thanks for her suggestions and understanding.

Cambridge, Massachusetts
March, 1975

CONTENTS

Altering Collective Bargaining

THE EMERGENCE AND
EVOLUTION OF
COLLECTIVE BARGAINING
IN PUBLIC EDUCATION

The widescale entrance of professional groups into the field of collective bargaining is largely a public sector phenomenon. It is in our judgement, the most important new development in American labor history since the organization of the mass production industries in the late 1930's. *

Over the last several years union organizing among public employees has been rapidly on the rise. Derek C. Bok and John T. Dunlop have characterized labor relations in the 1960s as the "decade of the public employee."[1] Indeed, Robert Helsby, the chairperson of the Public Employee Relations Board (PERB) in New York City, more recently said that the "advent of public sector relations represents one of the dynamic changes in our society," and it reveals that we are "rapidly becoming a negotiating society."[2]

Teacher organizations were very much a part of this public-employee decade. James Koerner has observed that one of the surprising phenomena of the 1960s was the "raucous rise of classroom teachers and their professional organizations."[3] Prior to 1960, for instance, few states had any laws dealing with the bargaining rights of teachers. By July 1974, however, 38 of the states were conducting some form of teacher negotiations under sanction of law.[4] This collective bargaining drive was spearheaded by the American Federation of Teachers (AFT), which at first was smaller and considerably more militant than the one-million-member National Education Association

---

*Scope of Bargaining in the Public Sector—Concepts and Problems (Washington, D.C.: U.S. Department of Labor, 1972), pp. 17-18.

(NEA). The NEA had consistently projected a professional posture
that rejected labor tactics and labor affiliation. Not surprisingly, in
the early 1960s the NEA opposed collective bargaining, but by the end
of the decade the differences between the NEA and the AFT became
very blurred, since the NEA had moved to adopt a stance similar to
that of the AFT. In fact, in October 1973 the two organizations began
detailed merger negotiations, clearly indicating that the rivalry was
about to end.* Negotiations regarding the merger of the two largest
teacher organizations in the country were broken off in early 1974, and
the election of Albert Shanker to the presidency of the AFT in August
1974 was expected to postpone a national merger. Nevertheless, there
are in existence several citywide mergers,† and the AFT and NEA
affiliates in New York State have already created a merged organization.

The emergence of collective bargaining on the part of teachers
resulted in an upheaval in public education. More specifically, this
upheaval came about because the teachers were seeking to legally end
unilateral decision-making on the part of boards of education and
school administrators; the existing educational power structure was
being militantly challenged by teachers through their union organizations. As Robert E. Doherty and Walter E. Oberer observed, "The
handwriting on school board walls is that of a changing of the guard in
public education. The traditional unilateral determination of [issues
of] strong consequence to teachers is passe."[5]

At the outset the teachers sought to end unilateral control over
their salary scale. A "changing of the guard" resulted in teacher demands for higher wages and improved fringe benefits, and "collective
bargaining rather than collective begging" became a common teacher-
union expression. Salary-related matters had top priority in the first
round of negotiations. A New York _Times_ reporter in early 1967, as
a wave of teacher militancy swept the country, pointed out that nearly
all authorities agreed that the teacher rebellion was rooted in deep-

----

*For some interesting observations about the external as well as
internal political implications of the merging of the AFT and NEA, see
Myron Lieberman, "The Union Merger Movement: Will 3,500,000
Teachers Put It All Together?" _Saturday Review_, June 24, 1973, pp.
50-55.

†Mergers, according to the December 1974 issue of the _Ameri-
can Teacher_ (p. 3), have occurred in Los Angeles, New Orleans, and
more recently Dade County, Florida. Interestingly, the merger in
Dade County has occurred since the national merger talks were broken
off. I would predict a merger on a national level within the next three
to five years.

seated dissatisfaction over salaries. [6] No matter what the union priorities, the fact was that a new structure of decision making was having its impact on the schools.

This trend toward bilateral decision making has been noted in a comprehensive report on public-sector bargaining sponsered by the U.S. Labor Department.

> We are rapidly moving from an era of unilateralism in public sector activity to one of bilateralism. This trend will undoubtedly continue at an accelerated rate. Consultation, negotiation and bargaining which result in a genuine redistribution of authority are becoming part of everyday management in the public sector. The group on the cutting edge of this revolution are the salaried professions. The implications of this revolution are a tall challenge to public management and employee organizations alike. [7]

Since the early 1960s this new form of bilateral decision making in public education has mushroomed as an increasing number of collective bargaining agreements have been negotiated. The teacher union movement has had a meteoric rise since the relatively militant United Federation of Teachers (UFT), an affiliate of the AFT, defeated the NEA in a collective bargaining election in New York City in December 1961. While such bargaining agreements were rare in the early 1960s, according to an NEA survey in 1966-67 there already were a total of 389 agreements covering some 208,000 teachers. By 1972-73 this had swelled to roughly 4,200 agreements covering 1.4 million teachers. This figure is certain to increase over the next few years. Too, increased organizing drives among college teachers will contribute to more collective bargaining agreements in education.

To deal with this development, among teachers in particular and public employees in general, by 1974 some 12 states had enacted comprehensive laws dealing with all state employees. At least another 26 have laws that are applicable to some public occupation categories. [8] It should be noted that to some degree state action was triggered by President John F. Kennedy's issuance of Executive Order 10988 on January 17, 1962, granting bargaining rights to federal employees. Indirectly this order had a positive impact on the teacher union movement, although it is true that it provided a new framework only for employee-management relations in the federal sector, since as one writer has observed, Kennedy's order generally "signified a change in attitude toward negotiations in the public sector." [9] One government report concluded that Executive Order 10988 was actually more significant for its impact on state and local government than for its effect on bargaining rights for federal employees, which were quite restricted. [10]

CHANGES IN THE SCOPE OF NEGOTIATIONS

The history of collective bargaining in public education has been well documented. * The focus here will be on new conflict areas that have emerged in the later stages of this history. As mentioned previously, from the beginning teachers unions were chiefly concerned, and rightfully so, with the plight of teacher salary schedules. Bargaining at the beginning seemed to conform in practice to federal legislation, which defined it as follows:

> the performance of the mutual obligation of the employer and the representatives of the employees to meet at reasonable times and confer in good faith with respect to wages, hours, and other terms and conditions of employment, or the negotiations of any agreement or any question arising thereunder, and the execution of a written contract incorporating any agreement reached if requested by either party, but such obligation does not compel either party to agree to a proposal or require making of any concession. [11]

Negotiations in most instances centered around salary, fringe benefits, grievance procedures, recognition, organizational rights, impasse resolutions, extra duty pay, and specific working conditions. Bargaining tended to focus on what has come to be known in labor relations parlance as "bread and butter" issues or "rates of pay, wages, hours of employment or other conditions of employment." This latter phrase comes directly from the National Labor Relations Act (NLRA), often referred to by some as labor's Magna Carta. This language from section 9(a) of the NLRA is often referred to as a definition of the

---

*For major analysis of the history and rise of teacher collective bargaining, see Myron Lieberman, The Future of Public Education (Chicago: University of Chicago Press, Phoenix Books, 1960); Michael H. Moskow and Myron Lieberman, Teachers and Unions (Philadelphia: University of Pennsylvania Press, 1968); Myron Lieberman and Michael H. Moskow, Collective Negotiations for Teachers (Chicago: Rand McNally and Co. , 1966); also see Michigan Law Review 67 (March 1969), entire issue, particularly Ida Klaus, "The Evolution of a Collective Bargaining Relationship in Public Education: New York City's Changing Seven-Year History," pp. 1033-66, and Charles R. Perry and Wesley A. Wildman, The Impact of Negotiations in Public Education: The Evidence from the Schools (Worthington, Ohio: Charles A. Jones Publishing Co. , 1970).

scope of bargaining. Simply put, scope of bargaining refers to the range of subjects that will be bargained over at the negotiations table.

Determining just what the scope of bargaining will be, both in the private and public sectors, has been, and continues to be, a major controversy. Harry H. Wellington and Ralph K. Winter indicate that, since the very beginning of American labor history, the scope of bargaining has remained a "vexing question."[12] Bok and Dunlop, in discussing the unionization of public employees in Labor and the American Community, stress that bargaining in the public sector will be largely influenced by the way in which several central issues are resolved over the next few years, and they list the scope of negotiations as one of the key issues.[13] Like these authors, Sterling Spero and John M. Capozzola contend that public employees have been able to bring about through collective bargaining a sharing with management in decisive powers affecting important areas of public policy; concluding that "while the strike is the most dramatic issue, equally important is the rising extent of co-determination of policy in the public administrative process, now widely referred to as participative decision making. The ultimate effect of these tendencies raises serious questions, the answers to which cannot be foreseen."[14] Referring specifically to education, Ronald G. Corwin suggests that the movement by teachers to determine educational policies of common concern can be boiled down to a question of who controls American education. To Corwin, "the issue is who should control, and at stake is the power structure of American education."[15] It should be clear that a change from unilateral decision making to a bilateral form of decision making has resulted in some redistribution of power, although this does not mean that in every circumstance teacher organizations have gained strength to a point at which there is now an equal balance of power between teachers and their employers.

The bargaining movement has arisen against a larger background of marked inequity in the distribution of power between these groups. For instance, a 1958 study by Robert Dahl, indicated that teachers were not a decisive part of the power structure in the New Haven school system. By studying eight different sets of decisions within the school system, Dahl found that there were three pivotal centers, either initiating or vetoing policies: the mayor's office, the board of education, and the superintendent.[16] While he also found that these three centers of power were "constrained in their choices by what they think will be acceptable to the teachers,"[17] on balance he concluded that teachers were not active participants in the decision-making process.

Furthermore, Corwin points out that Solomon and Eye in their 1961 study found that the contradiction between the teacher's role as a subordinate employee and the teacher as a professional was a crucial factor in explaining part of the cause for a "conflict of assertiveness."[18] In other words, despite their professional training, teachers ranked low in the hierarchial structure and did not have equal authority with the administration or school board.

In his own 1963-65 study of some 2,000 teachers and administrators in more than two dozen Midwestern public high schools, Corwin concluded that

> few teachers are initially involved in making policy decisions and although many of them report more control over routine decisions that come up in the classroom, it is fair to say that the vast majority of teachers want more control over their work. The majority of teachers believe that they should exercise the ultimate authority over major educational decisions and a handful are determined to increase their power, even at the risk of insubordination. [19]

Even after many risked acts of insubordination, and after much broader development of bargaining relationships, Alan Rosenthal in his 1969 study of five urban school systems* summarized the position of teachers as follows:

> However significant their progress recently, the power of teachers is today less than overwhelming. . . No doubt, their increased agitation has resulted in benefits they might otherwise have been denied. Yet, in contrast to the established governors of public education, teacher groups have little to say about educational policies, with the possible exception of salaries and related matters. [20]

In an article published in the same year, Don Wollett discussed more specific aspects of the continuing imbalance as follows:

> They [teachers] frequently lack a meaningful voice in determining the content of the courses they are teaching, or in selecting appropriate textbooks. Often they are not free to formulate their own lesson plans or to modify them if they do not produce desirable classroom response; seldom if ever, do they share a role in over-all curriculum planning. [21]

While these statements document the continuing imbalance, they also specify some of the reasons why teacher organizations have begun to

---

*Included in this study were the teacher organizations in Atlanta, San Francisco, Boston, Chicago, and New York.

encroach upon the making of policy. Even one of the more staunch
teacher union critics, Mario Fantini, has recently written that teachers were long the "economic and political doormat" of our public
school systems.

> The point has to be made repeatedly that teachers have
> been driven to organize and respond in this way. An un-
> responsive hierarchy in which each layer did its respec-
> tive job created unfair conditions for the teacher. Poor
> pay, no due process protection (so that arbitrary dis-
> missals were common), overloaded schedules, unrea-
> sonable control over the private life of the teacher, etc.,
> forced teachers to stick together in order to improve
> their lot and this sticking together has produced signifi-
> cant improvement for teachers. [22]

And yet, as we shall see later in this chapter and in Chapters 2
and 3, many developments have occurred that might significantly alter
the conclusions about teacher powerlessness that Rosenthal and Wollett
drew in 1969.

SCOPE AND BROADER POLITICAL ISSUES

Determining what is bargainable becomes a critical political
issue.* Bargaining in effect introduces a new focus of politics in

---

*A number of articles have appeared discussing the question of
the expansion of scope of bargaining as it relates to the electoral process. Robert E. Doherty, "Public Employee Bargaining and the Conferral of Public Benefits," Labor Law Journal 22 (August 1971): 485-
92; Kenneth McLennan and Michael H. Moskow, "Public Education,"
in Emerging Sectors of Collective Bargaining, edited by Seymour L.
Wolfbein (Braintree, Mass.: D.H. Mark Publishing, 1970); Harry H.
Wellington and Ralph K. Winter, Jr., "Structuring Collective Bargaining in Public Employment," Yale Law Journal 78 (June 1969): 1107-27;
David L. Kirp, "Collective Bargaining in Education: Professionals as
a Political Interest Group," Journal of Public Law 21 (1972): 323-38;
Jerome Lefkowitz, "Unionism in the Human Services Industries," Albany Law Review 36 (1972): 603-31; Clyde W. Summers, "Public Employee Bargaining: A Political Perspective," Yale Law Journal 83
(May 1974): 1156-1200; Robert L. Ridgley, "Collective Bargaining and
Community Involvement in Education: The Trouble with Negotiations,"
(mimeographed, Boston: League of Women Voters of Massachusetts,
1974).

education.* Roscoe Martin, for example, has defined politics as "the contest which develops around the definition and control of policy."[23] Applying his definition to public education, he said, "it may be said that the management of public schools in a significant sense is politics, for politics centers on the principal foci of decision making and public school administration is fundamentally a process in which decisions are arrived at and implemented."[24]

The controversial issue of formulating public school policy through bargaining is raised even more directly in a 1974 report in the Fordham Urban Law Journal.

Questions of public policy are clearly involved in teacher negotiations. The learning experiences of children and its effects upon the future ideas, philosophy and attitudes is essentially a political concern with control vested in the community, not in the hands of a small group of professionals.[25]

The above report goes on to raise the overriding concern of this thesis: the authors conclude that bargaining could "diminish the community's ability to fashion a public policy in educational matters."[26] This issue deeply troubles a large number of people active in public-sector bargaining today. As Arvid Anderson, chairperson of the New York City Office of Collective Bargaining, has said, "The task of public officials and public unions is to insure that the process works in the public interest."[27] People like Anderson are concerned about the public interest because they see public unions as seeking social change through the negotiations process as well as advancement of their economic and working conditions.

Anderson maintains that this interest in social change is revealed by "demands of teachers who want to bargain about the school curriculum or class size; welfare workers who want to bargain over the level of benefits to welfare recipients; nurses who wish to bargain about the number of duty stations; police who want to regulate the number of men on a patrol or their authority to make arrests."[28] To Anderson, there clearly are proper policy subjects for negotiations between the employer and employee, but he does not agree that the collective bargaining process is the appropriate means of resolving all major public policy questions.[29] From his prominent position in public sector bargaining, he has concluded that the issue of deciding public policy through

---

*For one view of this change in the political struggle for control of the schools, see Mario Fantini, What's Best for the Children: Resolving the Power Struggle between Parents and Teachers (New York: Doubleday, Anchor Press, 1974).

bargaining is "sharpest" in public education. This controversy is highlighted by a statement made by a member of the Seattle Board of Education, who maintains that "the primary reason for the erosion of local control is the imposition of collective bargaining in public education."[30]

To many, including this writer, neither the erosion of local control nor the loss of confidence in our public schools can be solely attributed to the rise of collective bargaining in public education; yet Fantini points out a significant development that warrants serious attention, as follows:

> Through many just struggles, educators especially teachers, have begun to achieve professional status and protection against political and sectarian denominations. Yet the scales must not tip toward a technocracy . . . in which the public, especially parents, cannot exercise the right to examine and help alter the professional process in education. [31]

It is not uncommon for teacher-union leaders and their allies to view remarks like Fantini's as being anti-union. Given the still somewhat infantile stage of bargaining in public education, it is not surprising that teachers unions see attempts to challenge their new-won power as just another guise for attempts to undermine bargaining completely.

THE RISE OF BILATERAL STRUCTURE

Concerns like those treated by Anderson and Fantini, as well as those of this study, raise fundamental questions about the evolving structure of policy determination. Paul Prasow's report on the scope of bargaining in the public sector points directly to this issue, as follows:

> It is perhaps not an overstatement to say that in planning for the years ahead the significant question is not whether salaried professionals will organize for purposes of engaging in direct negotiations with employers. The pertinent policy issues relate to the kinds of structure that will be created for the parties to carry out their bargaining functions. [32]

Similarly, Harry H. Wellington and Ralph K. Winter, in their book The Unions and The Cities, argue that the pertinent question is the method of participation by public employees in the shaping of public policy. [33]

In summary, then, collective bargaining became widespread in the public sector in general and in public education in particular, during the 1960s. The emergence of bargaining in the field of education introduced another power force, teachers, into the educational political arena. Collective bargaining, and with it the establishment of a bilateral relationship between employer and emplyee, has served to drastically alter the power structure in a vast number of public school systems.

It is important to note that at the same time that teachers were pushing for bargaining rights during the 1960s, the educational establishment came under severe attack from academicians and civil rights groups. Teacher organizations were in fact confronting a public institution that was having its broader legitimacy challenged, and it was no wonder that there was no immediate public outcry against teacher union demands calling for shared decision making, since those in power had lost credibility. In many instances the rhetoric of teacher groups echoed that of educational critics. Teachers, like many urban groups, particularly black groups, claimed they were powerless and oppressed by the educational system. Bargaining was a tool that could both advance the rights of teachers and improve the educational program. Indeed, it was not uncommon in the first stages of bargaining, which were the campaign for bargaining rights and the first contract negotiations, to find community and parent groups, particularly in urban communities, supporting the teachers in their efforts to gain new rights through bargaining agreements. *

However, there were some preliminary signs of community discontent with teacher bargaining, especially in black communities, even prior to the Ocean Hill-Brownsville strike in New York City. It was this latter event, however, that prompted many people to begin questioning the general direction of the teacher union movement. It is a mistake, though, to conclude that community control was the sole source of rising concern over the trend in teacher negotiations. As earlier indicated, the move on the part of teachers to become involved with what many called public policy issues also evoked concern from public officials, scholars, labor relations experts, and other community groups. Increased salaries and fringe benefits were generally considered reasonable bargaining demands; afterall, America, since the passage of the Wagner Act in 1935, had become accustomed to

---

*As a teacher union organizer in Michigan and later in Washington, D.C., I can verify that even during strike situations we often depended upon and received community support. This does not mean there was no community opposition to teacher organization; it is merely to say that at the formative stages there was no organized community resistance to the drive for teacher power.

these traditional labor demands; but when teachers began to press for an expansion of the scope of bargaining to include issues dealing with educational policies, an increasingly large number of people began to voice opposition.

The Prasow report referred to earlier, the questions and concerns posed by scholars like Wellington and Winter, and the views of Mario Fantini, a participant in the community control movement, generally reflect the views of many people who are seriously questioning the legitimacy of the collective bargaining structure as it now functions in public education. *

Because groups other than teachers and administrators are directly affected by the bargaining process, certain questions arise. Does a strict bilateral labor realtionship model based on the private-sector labor experience serve the public interest? Should the scope of teacher negotiations be simply restricted to salary and a limited number of working conditions? Does the community and/or its elected board of education really have an effective voice in the negotiating process? Will the current structure of bargaining offset the possibility and positive potential of community participation in educational decision making?†

In order to address questions such as these, it is important to understand in detail what is taking place in the vital area of scope of negotiations. In the next two chapters, several relevant aspects of the scope of negotiations are explored.

----

*It should be pointed out that the question of teacher strikes also troubled a number of these same critics. I do not mean to underestimate this concern, but overall, this study will not treat this question. A number of works adequately deal with the topic, including Harry H. Wellington and Ralph K. Winter, The Union and the Cities (Washington, D.C.: The Brookings Institution, 1971); and The Michigan Law Review 67 (March 1969), entire issue. For a view in support of the right of teachers to strike, see the concise article by David Selden, "Needed: More Teacher Strikes," Saturday Review, May 15, 1965.

†As was indicated in my earlier study, "The Scope of Teacher Negotiations in the Evolution and Development of the Collective Bargaining Process," (mimeographed, Cambridge, Mass.: Harvard University, 1974), little attention in the literature has been given this topic. However, one of the first reports dealing with this subject has been published, Seymour B. Sarason, Charles W. Cheng, Don Davies, The Community at the Bargaining Table (Boston, Institute for Responsive Education, 1975).

NOTES

1. Derek C. Bok and John T. Dunlop, Labor and the American Community (New York: Simon and Schuster, 1970), p. 313.

2. Robert D. Helsby, "Federal Law and Public Sector Bargaining," in "Symposium: Equity and Public Employment," Washington, D.C., May 29, 1974, p. 1 (Mimeographed.)

3. James D. Koerner, Who Controls American Education? (Boston: Beacon Press, 1968), p. 25.

4. William R. Hazard, "Courts in the Saddle: School Boards Out," Phi Beta Kappan, December 1974, p. 260.

5. Robert E. Doherty and Walter E. Oberer, Teachers, School Boards and Collective Bargaining: A Change of the Guard (Ithaca: New York State School of Industrial and Labor Relations, Cornell University, 1967), p. 89.

6. David R. Jones, "Militancy Sweeping U.S. Schools as Dissatisfied Teachers Turn to Strikes," New York Times, June 21, 1967, p. 85.

7. Paul Prasow, Archie Kleingartner, Edwin H. Kaye, Howard S. Block, et al., Scope of Bargaining in the Public Sector: Concepts and Problems (Washington, D.C.: U.S. Department of Labor, 1972), p. 53.

8. Helsby, op. cit., p. 3.

9. Robert H. Chanin, "Negotiations in Public Education: Developing a Legislative Framework" National Education Association (Washington, D.C.: ERIC Document Reproduction, 033479, 1969), p. 3.

10. Prasow, op. cit., p. 57.

11. The National Labor Relations Act, Section 8(d).

12. Harry H. Wellington and Ralph K. Winter, Jr., "The Limits of Collective Bargaining in Public Employment," Yale Law Journal 78 (June 1969): 1107-1127.

13. Bok and Dunlop, op. cit., p. 320.

14. Sterling Spero and John M. Capozzola, The Urban Community and Its Unionized Bureaucracies: Pressure Politics in Local Government Labor Relations (New York: Dunellen Publishing, 1973), p. 325.

15. Ronald G. Corwin, Militant Professionalism: A Study of Organizational Conflict in High Schools (New York: Appleton-Century-Crofts, 1970), p. 48.

16. Robert A. Dahl, Who Governs? (New Haven: Yale Paperbacks, 1961), p. 150.

17. Ibid., p. 155.

18. Corwin, op. cit., p. 46.

19. Ibid., p. 343.

20. Alan Rosenthal, Pedagogues and Power: Teacher Groups in School Politics (Syracuse: Syracuse University Press, 1969), p. 175.

21. Don H. Wollett, "The Coming Revolution in Public School Management," Michigan Law Review 67 (March 1969): 1020.

22. Mario Fantini, What's Best for the Children? Resolving the Power Struggle between Parents and Teachers (New York: Doubleday, Anchor Press, 1974), pp. 100-01.

23. Roscoe C. Martin, Government and the Suburban School (Syracuse: Syracuse University Press, 1962), p. 52.

24. Ibid., p. 53.

25. "Teacher Collective Bargaining—Who Runs the Schools?" Fordham Urban Law Journal 2 (1973-74): 508.

26. Ibid., p. 508.

27. Arvid Anderson, "The Impact of Public Sector Bargaining: An Essay Dedicated to Nathan P. Fensinger," reprint, Wisconsin Law Review, 1973, p. 995.

28. Arvid Anderson, "School Policy and Collective Bargaining," mimeographed (Madison: University of Wisconsin, 1973), pp. 1-2.

29. Ibid., p. 2.

30. Robert L. Ridgley, "Collective Bargaining and Community Involvement in Education: The Trouble with Negotiations" (mimeographed, Boston: League of Women Voters of Massachusetts, 1974), p. 1.

31. Fantini, op. cit., p. 6.

32. Prasow, op. cit., p. 42.

33. Harry H. Wellington and Ralph K. Winter, Jr., The Unions and the Cities (Washington, D.C.: The Brookings Institution, 1971), p. 24.

2

THE SCOPE OF
NEGOTIATIONS:
LEGISLATIVE AND
LEGAL DEFINITIONS

We place no limit on the items which are subject to the
bargaining process. Anything on which the two parties
can agree should become a part of the agreement. Anything on which they cannot agree will not appear. *

There is general agreement among those most familiar with
teacher negotiations that during the last few years there has been a
widening of bargainable issues. Expansion of the scope of negotiations
has meant that some teacher unions have gained access to educational
policy making. As I pointed out in Chapter 1, a number of observers
of public-sector collective bargaining are greatly disturbed by this
development. They seem especially to fear that public unions in general, and teacher unions in particular, will subvert the traditional
political processes by securing disproportionate and unchecked power
through the essentially closed institution of collective bargaining. The
issue is not nearly that simple, however. The heart of the dilemma
has been summarized by Jerome Lefkowitz, deputy chairperson of
New York's Public Employment Relations Board (PERB), as follows:

The problem is not one of right against wrong. The interest of professional and other employees in the human
services industries in negotiations over their terms and

_____

*Charles Cogen, Former President, The American Federation
of Teachers, Negotiations Manual, Department of Collective Bargaining, American Federation of Teachers, p. E. 1.

conditions of employment is legitimate and vital. The
mission and effectiveness of their employment is often
involved in decisions affecting those terms and conditions of employment. Other community groups also have
legitimate and vital interests in decisions which affect
the mission and efficiency of these agencies. It is important that the interest of the employees and the interest of other community groups be protected, one in harmony with the other. The challenge is to find a way to
do so. [1]

Lefkowitz poses the question of representing the public interest,
a question that still remains unanswered in the field of teacher negotiations. The scope problem is more pronounced in school bargaining
than in any other area. This fact was especially noted in the Paul Prasow study, as follows:

There is a marked broadening in the scope of negotiations
for public school teachers when compared with virtually
any other classification of employee, public or private.
It is widely recognized that the status of teachers as professionals gives them a legitimate concern as to educational objectives and professional standards. [2]

More importantly, the report goes on to note, "This element of
'professionalism' introduces concepts and issues that are simply not
found at other levels or types of employment. As a result, it seems
likely that the most dramatic changes in traditional bargaining concepts
will take place in teacher negotiations."[3]
     It is important to show how states and other legal institutions
have taken steps to protect the public interest and to prepare for the
"dramatic changes in traditional bargaining concepts" that result from
the expansion of the scope of negotiations. These questions and others
of a similar nature are explored below: first there is a review of the
ways in which a few states have attempted to handle the scope issue
in legislation; this is followed by a review of certain pertinent legal
cases related to the scope of bargaining.

STATE LAWS: SCOPE REMAINS A VEXING QUESTION*

---

*Not all state statutes will be covered in this section. A number
of readings provide a comprehensive review of state statutes and the

One writer has argued that the failure to create national machinery to govern labor relations in teacher negotiations has not fostered mature collective bargaining that would meet the needs of teachers.[4] To date, any such national legislation that would govern collective bargaining in public education has not been enacted.† However, legislative

---

status of the law: Paul Prasow, Archie Kleingartner, Edwin H. Kaye, Howard S. Block, et al., Scope of Bargaining in the Public Sector: Concepts and Problems (Washington, D.C.: U.S. Department of Labor, 1972), see Appendix I, II, III; Arvid Anderson, "The Impact of Public Sector Bargaining: An Essay Dedicated to Nathan P. Fensinger," Reprint, Wisconsin Law Review, 1973, p. 995; Lee C. Shaw, "The Development of State and Federal Laws," in Public Workers and Public Unions, edited by Sam Zagoria (Englewood Cliffs, N.J.: Prentice-Hall, 1972); Robert G. Howlett, "Where We've Been and Where We Are: History and Nature of Collective Bargaining in the United States," Equity and the Public Employee—A Symposium, Washington, D.C., March 25, 1974 mimeographed; Irving H. Sabghir, The Scope of Bargaining in Public Sector Collective Bargaining (Albany: New York State Public Employment Relations Board, 1970); Carl J. Megel, A Guide for Legislative Action and State Collective Bargaining Laws (Washington, D.C.: American Federation of Teachers, 1974).

†There are two major bills before the 94th Congress that seek a federal bargaining law to cover all public employees. One bill, which is supported by the American Federation of Teachers (AFT), essentially calls for bringing all public employees under the National Labor Relations Act. The other bill, which is being advanced by the Coalition of American Public Employees (CAPE), seeks a separate federal law covering public employees. Given the alleged liberal climate of Congress, it is possible that one of these bills could be enacted within the next two years. In the fall of 1974, the American Federation of State, County and Municipal Employees (AFSCME), a dominant influence in CAPE, said it would be willing to support that AFT position. Albert Shanker, president of the AFT, was apparently surprised by AFSCME's willingness to change its stance, and actually, it appears the AFT may decrease its lobbying effort, since passage of a federal bill at this time would give the National Education Association (NEA) the upper hand in organizational strength in most states. Instead Sahnker is shifting the AFT position toward consolidating mergers between the NEA and the AFT at the city and state levels. After a large enough power base is secured by the AFT, then it should go all out for federal legislation. In any case, the internal politics on this issue within the AFL-CIO should be carefully watched over the next several months. For a

efforts to deal collective bargaining with teachers, as well as with other public employees, have been made on the state level. Action taken thus far does not disclose any consistent pattern by the states, especially with respect to the scope of negotiations.

Many of the state statutes require that the parties bargain with respect to wages, hours, and other terms and conditions of employment. Commenting on such statutes, Arvid Anderson, writing in the Wisconsin Law Review, has observed that "under such statutes it seems apparent that the meaning of the duty to bargain in the public sector will evolve gradually as it is more specifically defined by state agencies responsible for administering bargaining statutes, courts responsible for interpreting them and the parties themselves."[5]

In the field of education, Anderson underscores the fact that a few state legislatures specifically provide for a broad meaning of scope in teacher negotiations. Alaska's law, for instance, says the state board on behalf of state operated schools "shall negotiate" with its certified staff, "in good faith in matters pertaining to their employment and the fulfillment of their professional duties."[6] A statute in Kansas is similar in that it permits teacher groups the right "to participate in professional negotiations with boards of education . . . for the purpose of establishing, maintaining, protecting or improving terms and conditions of professional service."[7] New York State, a leader in public employee bargaining patterns, simply defines scope within the broad area of terms and conditions of employment. *

The Washington State statute specifically allows a broad range of subjects that are often associated with the function of policy making. Among the subjects cited as being bargainable are curriculum, textbook selection, in-service training, student teaching programs,

----

concise review of bills before the 94th Congress that pertain to public employees, see Ronald W. Haughton, "What the Federal Government Proposes on Collective Bargaining for Public Employees," Equity and Public Employment—A Symposium, Washington, D.C., March 25, 1974, (mimeographed), and Arnold Weber, "The Federal Dragon and the State Knights: The Role of Federal Law in Public Sector Bargaining," Equity and Public Employment—A Symposium, Washington, D.C., March 25, 1974, (mimeographed).

*It should be noted that New York City, in addition to falling under the jurisdiction of the state statute, the Taylor Law, has a city law that restricts the scope of negotiations, New York City Administrative Code 1173-4.3b (1973). As will be seen elsewhere, the UFT, which comes under this law, is considered by many to represent the epitome of teacher union power in the area of policy making.

personnel, hiring and assignment practices, leaves of absence, salaries and salary schedules, and noninstructional duties. [8]

The Connecticut statute, in addressing itself specifically to teacher negotiations, provides wide interpretation of what is bargainable; it says in part that the "board of education and the [teacher] organization have . . . the duty to negotiate with respect to salaries and other conditions of employment about which either party wishes to negotiate and such duty shall include the obligation . . . to meet at reasonable times, including meetings appropriately related to the budget-making process and confer in good faith with respect to salaries and other conditions of employment." [9]

However, it is clear that the Connecticut statute also has not resolved the matter, as revealed by a court ruling. In December 1971 the Connecticut Supreme Court in the case of West Hartford Education Association v. Dayson Decourcy, et al. ruled that mandatory subjects of bargaining include such matters as class size, teacher work load, binding arbitration of grievances, and the salaries and working conditions of teachers assigned to extracurricular activities. However, the court went on to say that matters pertaining to educational policy should be left to the discretion of the board of education. [10]

In Michigan, where teacher collective bargaining became widespread with the passage of a collective bargaining statute in 1965, the law again provides no definitive answer with respect to the scope of negotiations. Under the Michigan law, the Michigan State Mediation Board or the state courts can determine bargainable subjects. Employee groups can file an unfair labor practice charge with the board, claiming that certain matters are free to be negotiated. On the other hand, the employer or citizens can go to court, claiming that certain subjects should not be negotiated. [11] In a case that came before the Michigan State Labor Mediation Board, the trial examiner ruled that a wide range of subjects could be deemed mandatory subjects of bargaining, while in the same year (1966) a Michigan Circuit Court in a separate school district case ruled against the teacher union, which was seeking to expand the scope, suggesting that there was a very narrow range of bargainable items. [12]

Several states have attempted to resolve the scope question through restrictive legislation. For instance, Hawaii appears to have a very restrictive statute; under its law it is illegal for an employer and a labor organization to include in a collective bargaining agreement provisions that

> interfere with the right of the public employer to direct
> its employees, to set qualifications, standards for work,
> the nature and content of examinations; to suspend, de-
> mote, discharge or take other disciplinary action against

its employees for proper cause; to relieve an employee
from work for failure to perform or other legitimate
reasons; to maintain operational efficiency in government,
and to determine methods, means and personnel by which
the employer's operations are to be conducted. [13]

It has been ruled, nevertheless, that class size is a mandatory subject for bargaining, although this subject is often considered to be in
the realm of policy making.

Here it is worth stressing that Hawaii also grants public employees the right to strike, after exhausting state machinery. Where
strikes are legal, legislation tends to limit the scope. Indeed, the
language of the Hawaii statute seemingly subscribes to the point of
view held by Derek C. Bok and John T. Dunlop, who hold that if public
employees have the right to strike, then the scope of what can be negotiated ought to be limited. Where the right to strike does not exist,
then Bok and Dunlop believe that the scope of negotiations should be
broader, although they contend that the scope might still be somewhat
narrower in the event that certain matters either fall under management prerogatives or can seemingly be better resolved through the
political process. [14] Hawaii also calls for the parties to meet and confer in advance of the employer's budget-making process. Dupont and
Tobin argue that this language means that both parties must "weigh
educational policies against the cost of implementation and . . . make
a determination of the priorities involved. "[15]

The Pennsylvania Public Employee Relations Act states that public employers are not obligated to bargain over "matters of inherent
managerial policy. "[16] Nevertheless, the act does require the employers "to meet with employees to discuss policy matters affecting wages,
hours and terms and conditions of employment as well as the impact
thereon. "[17] It is important to note, however, that the Pennsylvania
statute does grant public employees the right to strike after exhausting the appropriate appellate machinery set up under the act. *

Oregon has a restrictive statute, by which the scope of mandatory bargaining in teacher negotiations is limited to salaries, grievance procedure, extra compensation, and related economic policies. [18]
Nevada's statute governing all public employees is strikingly similar
to that of Hawaii. [19] Pennsylvania, Vermont, and Wisconsin, have

---

*As will be indicated in Chapter 4, despite this legislative pro-
tection of management prerogatives, the scope of bargaining has expanded so greatly that a citizen group in Philadelphia has sued to restrict the school board and the union from subverting the public interest through the negotiation of policy questions with the teachers.

management rights clauses, which tend to restrict the scope of negotiations. Maine and Minnesota also attempted to exclude educational policy from the bargaining process.[20] The Maine statute is quite clear:

> School boards are required to confer and negotiate in good
> faith with respect to wages, hours, working conditions
> and contract grievance arbitration . . . [and to] meet and
> consult but not negotiate with respect to educational poli-
> cies[;] for the purpose of this paragraph, educational pol-
> icies shall not include wages, hours, working conditions
> or contract grievance arbitration.[21]

The Montana law has restrictive language similar to that of Maine, and it explicitly excludes from the scope of bargaining in grades K through 12 "matters of curriculum, policy of operation, selection of teacher and other personnel or physical plant."[22]

It is noteworthy that the Maine statute calls for consultation between teachers and the board on policy matters. Teacher unions have opposed consultation, essentially holding that consultation is nothing more than the benevolent paternalism that existed in many school systems prior to collective bargaining. In reality, consultation does not ultimately threaten the power balance. California's law seems to bear this out: in California, where consultation does exist, there is an extremely broad view of what can be discussed, but not negotiated, including

> all matters relating to employment conditions and em-
> ployer-employee relations and . . . with regard to all
> matters relating to the definition of educational objec-
> tives, the determination of the content of courses and
> curriculum, the selection of textbooks, and other aspects
> of the instructional program to the extent such matters
> are within the direction of the public school employer.[23]

Finally, we can look for evolution in the definition of scope by examining two more recent statutes. In 1973 Massachusetts enacted a collective bargaining statute dealing with public employees; this statute does not give teachers or public employees the right to strike, nor in the case of teachers does it spell out in any detail the scope of negotiations. From the language in Section 6 it appears as though the parties themselves will determine what is bargainable at the negotiating table. *

---

*The Massachusetts Act also allows for a grievance procedure "culminating in final and binding arbitration to be invoked in the event of any dispute concerning the interpretation or application of such

In accordance with Section 6, the parties

> shall meet at reasonable times, including meetings in
> advance of the employer's budget-making process and
> shall negotiate in good faith with respect to wages, hours,
> standards of productivity and performance, and any other
> terms and conditions of employment, but such obligation
> shall not compel either party to agree to a proposal or
> make a concession. [24]

In Indiana the bargaining act of 1973 states that there are mandatory subjects requiring school employer and employees to bargain over
"salary, wages, and salary and wage related fringe benefits." However,
the statute further notes that negotiations can cover a wide range of
permissive subjects, including such items as curriculum development
and review; textbook selection; teaching methods; selection assignment
or promotions."* In his review of this act, however, Grant F. Shipley
has argued that the legislature did not resolve the scope question.

> To preserve school board responsiveness to community
> interests, the scope of bargaining is restricted by

----

written agreement." Thus, if the parties agreed to language calling
for teacher decision making in the area of staff development and evaluation and the board of education, then during the implementation stage
of the contract it could be protested by the employer on the grounds
that the provision meant consultation rather than decision making, and
the union could take the case to arbitration. In effect, a final interpretation of a specific provision regarding the operational aspect of the
scope of negotiations could be determined by an arbitrator. This would
not necessarily result in any definitive opinion on what is bargainable,
since the arbitrator would be confined to the specific contractual provision being raised by the union. Such a ruling, on the other hand,
might well have implications for future negotiations, insofar as it indicates what is bargainable. This could be the outcome regardless of
how the decision has gone for either party. Here it should be mentioned that administrators and board negotiators often fear that a board
grievance procedure leading to binding arbitration could give teachers
a greater say in shaping educational policy.

*For an in-depth discussion of this Indiana statute and related
questions of scope, see Grant F. Shipley, "Determining the Scope of
Bargaining under Indiana's Education Employment Relations Act,"
Indiana Law Journal 49 (Spring 1974): 460-81.

statutory reservations of management rights. Problems
arise, however, because disputed items may fall within
the definitional ambit of both the bargaining rights clause
and management rights provisions. [25]

Shipley then concludes as follows:

Unable to draw a precise line between what should be
deemed bargainable and nonbargainable items and unwilling to formulate a clear rule that would always favor one
provision over the other, the legislature has created
problems of ambiguity which courts and boards must
resolve by applying the statutory accomodations of interests to diverse fact situations. [26]

It is apparent that, even after a decade of teacher bargaining,
the Indiana statute indicates the difficulty, and to some the failure, of
legislation to resolve the scope of negotiations questions adequately.
This review of legislation indicates plainly that state action does not
provide any general guide or consistent framework.

   This is probably because there are disagreements not only over
what state laws should contain, but also because some authorities reject the notion that the scope of negotiations should be defined in any
legislation at all. Robert H. Chanin, the chief legal counsel for the
NEA, argues that legislation that attempts to clearly define the scope
of bargaining could lead to unworkable inflexibility. In Chanin's view,

experience in the private sector indicates that it may well
be impossible to develop precise statutory definition and
that the metes and bounds of negotiability can come only
through the very process of ad hoc dispute and decision
that is now being experienced. [27]

Also, in a 1974 issue of Changing Education, the official publication
of the AFT, Charles Miller expresses a viewpoint similar to that of
Chanin:

The future scope of contract discussions and provisions
will depend not so much on legislative fiat as upon the
strength and skill of the bargainers on both sides of the
table . . . . Any attempt to establish general guidelines
suitable in many situations will be futile because each
situation must be dealt with in terms of particular power
and leadership. [28]

Albert Shanker, President of the AFT and the UFT, sums up the general outlook of teacher unions and suggests disputable mutually beneficial outcomes as follows:

> Our American tradition favors letting the employees and the employers fight it out among themselves, whatever decision they reach, both parties will concur—both parties can view the results of their negotiations affirmatively. [29]

Finally, Wollett has argued that the whole debate is "much ado about nothing." His contention is that if the management negotiator is intent on "building a reputation as a protagonist of ordered government and managerial sovereignty the issue of what is bargainable is fertile ground." On the other hand, he adds, "if the negotiator approaches the table with the intent of resolving problems rather than identifying barriers that prevent a negotiated settlement then the issue of the scope of bargaining is of little importance. "[30]

It is clear that state legislation will continue to fail to resolve the scope controversy. The point bears repeating, that given the failure to delineate scope, the question of other community interests being represented in the determination of educational policies is left unanswered. Outside the legislative process, efforts have been made to determine what is bargainable on a case-by-case basis; I will turn to several important legal cases dealing with the scope of bargaining in public education.

SCOPE: A LOOK AT THE LEGAL RECORD

Scope in the private sector, as interpreted by the National Labor Relations Board and upheld by the Supreme Court, falls into two categories of bargaining. In the first instance, bargaining is required to demonstrate good faith with respect to wages, hours, and working conditions. This has been referred to as the mandatory bargaining area. In the second instance, bargaining is not required of either party but upon voluntary agreement of both parties certain subjects can be negotiated. [31] This is commonly known as the permissive area of bargaining. This rule of thumb, which was developed in the private sector, is now being used in some locations to determine the scope of teacher negotiations.

What is mandatory and what is permissive often goes to the heart of the problem of determining just what can be included in the negotiated agreement. The experience in New York in dealing with this issue is well worth considering, since it provides some important insights into the structure of the bargaining relationship in public education. * Upon analysis of the Taylor Law, Kurt L. Hanslowe and Walter E. Oberer concluded that the scope of negotiations might well be broader than the previously exercised unilateral employer authority. [32] They underlined what they considered to be the critical role of PERB in this area in this way: "The Taylor Law . . . places upon PERB the duty to determine in the first instance subject to judicial review, the scope of negotiability when the issue is presented in refusal to negotiate cases. "[33] They added that "PERB should make its own fresh analysis of the issue of preemption and decide it on the basis of the soundest public employment policy permitted by competing law, having in mind, of course, that its decision will be subject to judicial review. "[34]

Some of PERB's decisions since 1971 reveal that in education at least it is taking a posture similar to the one advocated by Hanslowe and Oberer. In two major decisions made by PERB, for example, the scope of bargaining was restricted. However, while management was upheld in refusing to negotiate over a specific policy, the impact of management's decision was ruled bargainable. For instance, in a case involving the New Rochelle Federation of Teachers, PERB upheld a board decision to reduce the budget, resulting in the layoff of some librarians. Nevertheless, PERB also held that while management could initiate the layoffs, the right of the teachers involved to bargain for other positions, severance benefits, and additional matters was a proper subject for the bargaining table. [35] Guiding PERB's determination of a management prerogative

---

*Since New York is one of the more advanced states in this area of labor management realtions in the public sector, this section will tend to emphasize developments in New York. This does not mean that what occurs in New York necessarily will have an impact on how other states cope with the scope issue. Nevertheless, the experience in New York is important, and frequently trends in New York do affect other states. With the merger of the NEA and AFT in New York, it is possible that the direction taken by the union as well as that of PERB will have a significant influence beyond the borders of the Empire State. For an analysis of the role of PERB in determining the scope of bargaining under the Taylor Law, see the discussion by Kurt L. Hanslowe and Walter E. Oberer, "Determining the Scope of Negotiations under Public Employment Relations Statutes," Industrial and Labor Relations Review 24 (April 1971): 432-41.

was the concept that basic decisions as to public policy
should not be made in the isolation of a negotiation table,
but rather should be made by those having the direct and
sole responsibility therefor, and whose actions in this
regard are subject to review in the electoral process. "[36]

In the other case, the West Irondequoit Teachers Association
decision, PERB ruled that the matter of class size was a fundamental
question of educational policy; therefore it was not a mandatory subject for bargaining. Again, the impact of such a decision must be bargained over. However, PERB's language in the case is clear, but the
scope issue in part was still left to the parties to decide.

It is not the thrust of this decision that an employer is
not required to negotiate on subjects which affect the
allocation of resources because salaries clearly have
such an effect, rather the thrust of this decision and
the decision in the New Rochelle case is that basic policy
decisions as to the implementation of a mission of an
agency of government are not mandatory subjects of
negotiations. [37]

PERB left little doubt that class size was a permissive subject.
"We would make it clear that this decision does not prohibit negotiations on class size. "[38] The majority went on to say that there was
definitely a thin line between "a basic policy decision and the impact
on terms and conditions of employment. " PERB's decision in the West
Irondequoit Teachers case was later sustained by the New York Court
of Appeals. [39] However, this decision has not resulted in the elimination of such provisions from contracts. In 1974, for instance, the
Fordham Urban Law Journal found that well over half the negotiated
agreements in New York contained class-size articles. [40]

It is to be noted, however, that in a landmark case, Board of
Education vs. Huntington Associated Teachers, the New York Court
of Appeals held that PERB was in violation of the Taylor Law for refusing to negotiate on grievance arbitration for tenured teachers,
tuition reimbursement, teacher property damage, and a salary increase preceding retirement. The high court's language was unmis-
takably clear:

Under the Taylor Law, the obligation to bargain as to all
terms and conditions of employment is a broad and un-
qualified one, and there is no reason why the mandatory
provision of that act should be limited, in any way, except in cases where some other applicable statutory

provision explicitly and definitively prohibits the public
employer from making an agreement as to a particular
term or condition. . . .

Were it otherwise, a school board would have a
hard time bargaining effectively with its teachers concerning terms of employment, since it would frequently
be difficult, if not impossible, to find any particular
subject.

Public employers must be presumed to possess the
broad powers needed to negotiate with employees as to
all terms and conditions of employment.

It is hardly necessary to say that, if the Board
asserts a lack of power to agree to any particular term
or condition of employment, it has the burden of demonstrating the existence of a specific statutory provision
which circumscribes the exercise of such power.[41]

The Huntington case can be viewed as solidly endorsing the principles of an open agenda for collective bargaining. Anderson has placed
the decision in this context:

This kind of reasoning should put another nail in the cof-
fin of Dillon's rule which was the legal citation for the
excuse by which government lawyers, including school
lawyers, would figure out how not to do things. Dillon's
rule meant that unless a particular course of conduct was
specifically authorized by statute it was prohibited. In my
view, such reasoning is totally against the public interest
which at the same time endorses a policy of collective
bargaining. Unions are not hobbled by that kind of restrictive thinking. Whether it is wise to take a particular action is another matter, but that freedom to do so exists is
the message of Huntington and in my view sound doctrine.[42]

On the other hand, there may be other implications of this case. The
court may have opened the door for the state legislature to "explicitly
and definitively" bar certain items from the negotiating table, a move
that the legislature has not been prone to take in the past.

In May 1974, in Yorktown Faculty Association and Yorktown
Central School District, PERB held that the following were not mandatory subjects of negotiations: the employer's decision to eliminate
jobs; demands for a greater role in the making of decisions relating to

the development of curriculum; the evaluation of principals; the assignment of paraprofessionals and other educational matters; demands for
a greater role in the formulation of policy relating to student guidance
in high school; demands that each student have a specific number of
contact periods in various subject areas with teaching specialists; and
demands concerning the salary and job assignments of per diem sub-
stitutes who are not in the negotiating unit.[43] However, in the same
case, PERB ruled that the issue of "weighted student contact minutes
per week" (WSCM) was a mandatory negotiable item. Referring to its
decision in Matter of West Irondequoit Board of Education, PERB
stated as follows:

> In that decision we distinguished between matters of edu-
> cation policy that are not terms and conditions of employ-
> ment, such as class size, and the impact of such decisions
> on terms and conditions of employment, such as teacher
> workload. Class size is but one factor in the calculation
> of WSCM; a demand for limitations on WSCM is a work-
> load demand and a mandatory subject of negotiations. The
> formula for the determination of WSCM includes not only
> class size, but also hours of work and the number of
> teaching periods which are ruled mandatory subjects of
> negotiations in Matter of West Irondequoit Board of
> Education.[44]

To further the purpose of this study, a letter was sent to PERB asking
the following question:

> Do you see this case in any way leading to any restriction
> on the scope of bargaining in teacher negotiations in New
> York or would you consider Yorktown simply as an indivi-
> dual case having no significant implications for the scope
> of bargaining in general?[45]

Jerome Lefkowitz, the Deputy Chairperson of PERB, responded as
follows:

> It is my opinion that decisions restricting scope of
> negotiations will have significant but limited implications
> for scope of bargaining in general. In large measure
> collective bargaining is a confrontation of power, albeit
> a confrontation that is regulated by legal and administra-
> tive procedures. Decisions relating to scope of negotia-
> tions constitute such regulations. Where a union's mani-
> festations of power and its determination are sufficiently

strong, administrative and legal regulation are particularly great, administrative procedures restricting scope
of negotiations may be unnecessary. In the many situations where the power of the parties is in relative equilib-
rium, a decision that a demand is not a mandatory subject
of negotiations diverts the thrust of the negotiations into
other directions. [46]

In short, Lefkowitz does not see Yorktown as being any more
significant than any other case, and I conclude from this reply that
PERB will continue to deal with scope on a case-by-case basis. Given
the substance of Lefkowitz's response, it would appear that in many
circumstances increasingly more subjects that are not mandatory will
be included in bargaining contracts, that the scope will expand. Indeed
a report, "Teacher Collective Bargaining—Who Runs the Schools,"
in the Fordham Urban Law Journal concluded "that New York favored
a broad definition of the permissible scope of bargaining. It is the public policy of New York to include not to exclude, questionable terms
and conditions. "[47]

Another important ruling is to be noted in Matter of Board of
Higher Education of the City of New York and Professional Staff Congress. In this case PERB alludes to the role of other interest groups
in higher education governance outside the employer and employee.
"Collective negotiations," PERB states, "is a valuable technique to
resolve questions between employer and its employees concerning
terms and conditions of employment. It is not designed to resolve policy questions regarding the structure of governance of a public employer or the nature of the public employee's responsibility to its constituency. Questions in the latter category often involve issues of social
concern to many groups within the community other than the public
employer's administrative apparatus and its employees. "[48]

Finally, in its 1973 annual report, in order to offer a comprehensive view of the status of the scope issue, PERB listed the subjects
for negotiation that to date have been found to be either mandatory or
nonmandatory. *

---

*Mandatory subjects: procedures for evaluating probationary or
untenured teachers; wages and hours; sabbatical leave; job duties; promotional procedures for employees; school calendar; length of work
year; impact on employees of reduction in work force; impact of modi-
fication of class size; tours of duty, except that the employer may uni-
laterally determine the number of employees required to be on duty at
specified periods of time; manpower requirements when related to

A recent ruling by the Oregon Public Employment Relations Board also expands the scope of bargaining in education. The Oregon PERB ruled that the new law does not prohibit negotiations on working conditions not specifically consulted on prior to the contract nor specifically alluded to it. Accordingly, PERB agreed that bargainable subjects could include preparation time, class size, checkoff, grievance procedure, binding arbitration, and length of contract. [49] Again, the concept of mandatory as opposed to permissive subjects constitutes the essence of this decision.

In September 1974 the NEA reported that the Nevada Government Employee Management Relations Board, which as seen earlier operates under a restrictive statute, had ruled that the hiring of nonteacher aides and preparation time for parent-teacher meetings could be negotiated. Not excluded from bargaining by the board were teacher evaluation of evaluators; assignment of aides; hiring and assignment of nurses; a minimum discretionary fund per teacher for instructional materials; matters dealing with field trips; and the number of librarians and their staffing and operations. [50]

Similarly, decisions rendered by the courts in Pennsylvania point toward a relatively narrow view of scope. The Commonwealth Court of Pennsylvania, an appellate court, ruled in 1973 that even when a bargaining proposal involves wages, hours, and conditions of employment, the "further and controlling question is whether the item also involves matters of inherent policy." [51] If the item falls into the latter category, then it is not bargainable. Arguing that boards of education were subject to the Public School Code of 1949, the court held that under the Public Employment Relations Act, (1) bargainable items are of a limited nature, and (2) any item of wages, hours, and other items and conditions of employment, if affected by policy determination, are not bargainable items. [52] Using this extremely narrow definition of

---

safety; parking fees at work locations when they are controlled by the employer; impact of a professional development plan that would constitute a basis for an annual evaluation and for reappointment.

Nonmandatory subjects: overall policies and mission of government; budget cuts and resultant economically motivated decision to reduce work force; numerical limitations on class size; agency shop; residency requirements; promotional policy for job titles not within the negotiating unit; initial employment qualifications; demand that work force not be reduced except by attrition or disciplinary charge for cause; seminar or conference designed to enrich the professional staff at which attendance is not compulsory; demand that supervisor be of a specified rank or grade. State of New York Public Employment Relations Board Annual Report (Albany: PERB, 1973), pp. 3042-49.

the scope of bargaining, the court ruled 21 contested demands to be nonmandatory subjects for bargaining. *

This past fall, a decision by the Pennsylvania Labor Relations Board (PLRB) that had expanded the scope of bargainable issues, was overturned by the Pennsylvania Court of Common Pleas. PLRB had made the following ruling: "Viewing the elimination of the paid teacher aides as an integral part of a plan to replace union personnel with non-union personnel, the school's actions are not matters of inherent managerial policy but rather are matters subject to collective bargaining, contrary to the school's contention otherwise."[53] The court

---

*These were as follows: 1. Availability of proper and adequate classroom instructional printed matter; 2. Provision for time during the school day for team planning of required innovative programs; 3. Timely notice of teaching assignments for the coming year; 4. Separate desks and lockable drawer space for each teacher in the district; 5. Cafeteria for teachers in the senior high school; 6. Elimination of the requirement that teachers perform nonteaching duties, such as but not limited to, hall duty, bus duty, lunch duty, and study hall and parking lot duties; 7. Elimination of the requirement that teachers teach or supervise two consecutive periods in two different buildings; 8. Elimination of the requirement that teachers substitute for other teachers during planning periods and of teaching in noncertificated subject areas; 9. Elimination of the requirement that teachers chaperone athletic activities; 10. Elimination of the requirement that teachers unpack, store, check, or otherwise handle supplies; 11. Provision that there shall be one night each week free for teachers association meetings; 12. Provision that a teacher will, without prior notice, have free access to his personnel file; 13. Permission for a teacher to leave the building at any time during the school day unless he has a teaching assignment; 14. Provision for special teachers of preparation time equal to that provided for other staff members; 15. Provision for maximum class sizes; 16. Provision that the teacher association will be consulted in determining the school calendar; 17. Provision that school will officially close at noon of the last day of classes for Thanksgiving, Christmas, and Spring and Summer vacation; 18. Provision that at least one-half of the time requested for staff meetings be held during the school day; 19. Provision that the present Tuesday afternoon conference with parents be abolished and teachers hold conferences with parents by appointment at a mutually convenient time; 20. Provision that secondary teachers not be required to teach more than 25 periods per week and have at least one planning period per day; and 21. Provision that elementary teachers shall have one period or fifteen minutes per day for planning purposes.

disagreed with PLRB and found that the district had not engaged in
an unfair labor practice.

As was indicated earlier, Michigan has determined scope largely
on a case-by-case basis. However, Harry Edwards, writing in the
Michigan Law Review, refers to a decision, involving the Westwood
Community Schools, that could be used by other states in defining the
scope of negotiations. The Michigan Employment Relations Commission
used the following two criteria in its determination: (1) Is the subject
of such vital concern to both labor and management that it is likely to
lead to controversy and industrial conflict? (2) Is collective bargaining
appropriate for resolving such issues?[54] Edwards contends that such
reasoning will lead to a general widening of scope, although, significantly, the decision was tied to a prohibition on strikes. According to
these criteria, where strikes are barred, no limitations should be
placed on what can be negotiated.

Overall, the evidence is still coming in from the states. There
is uneven development throughout the country. New York and Michigan
are two of the states that have had considerable experience with bargaining in public education. In these two states the scope question is
being resolved primarily by the parties at the table and the respective
public employment relations boards. Indeed, Edwards points out that
most of the scope expansion has come through decisions rendered by
state labor boards. Some states appear to be expanding the scope on a
select number of policy questions, while excluding others. Of those
states with bargaining laws, limited to those reviewed in this study,
Pennsylvania appears to be placing the narrowest interpretation on
scope.

One of more salient factors is the general acceptance of the notion of mandatory and permissive subjects for negotiations. Application of this private-sector principle to bargaining in education is the
hallmark of the New Rochelle case cited above. The impact of the decision and the principles are clear. "If an issue is defined as being within educational policy and therefore permissive, the school board can
legally refuse even to discuss it. On the other hand, if the school board
wishes to discuss an educational policy issue. the Taylor Law empow-
ers the board to enter a binding agreement on it with the teachers.[55]

This concept of mandatory as opposed to permissive subjects
appears, whether explicitly set forth or not, to be the standard em-
ployed in a number of jurisdictions. Nowhere is this made clearer
than in the bargaining agreements themselves. The next chapter looks
at several contractual provisions, to gain insight into what is actually
negotiated. In short, what has been the practical impact of state laws
as well as of decisions by the state labor boards and the courts on
scope of bargaining?

NOTES

1. Jerome Lefkowitz, "Unionism in the Human Services Industries," Albany Law Review 36 (1972): 631.

2. Paul Prasow, Archie Kleingartner, Edwin H. Kaye, Howard S. Block, et al., Scope of Bargaining in the Public Sector: Concepts and Problems (Washington, D.C.: Department of Labor, 1972), p. 65.

3. Ibid., p. 65.

4. Ross A. Engle, "Teacher Negotiation: History and Comment," Journal of Public Law and Education 1 (July 1972): 487.

5. Arvid Anderson, "The Impact of Public Sector Bargaining: An Essay Dedicated to Nathan P. Fensinger," reprint, Wisconsin Law Review, 1973, p. 1,000.

6. Cited in Arvid Anderson, "School Policy and Collective Bargaining," mimeographed (Madison: University of Wisconsin, 1973).

7. Ibid., p. 4.

8. Ralph P. Dupont and Robert D. Tobin, "Teacher Negotiations into the Seventies," William and Mary Law Review 12 (Summer 1971): 721.

9. Ibid., p. 720.

10. Jeannette Feely, "The Scope of Bargaining: Recent Effects of the Teacher Union Movement on Policy Matters in Public Education" (mimeographed, Amherst: University of Massachusetts, 1973).

11. Charles T. Schmidt, Jr., Hyman Parker, and Bob Repas, A Guide to Collective Negotiations in Education (East Lansing: The School of Labor and Industrial Relations, Michigan State University, 1967), pp. 56-57.

12. Ibid., pp. 58-59.

13. Donald H. Wollett, "The Bargaining Process in the Public Sector: What Is Bargainable?" Oregon Law Review 51 (1971-72): 181-82.

14. Derek C. Bok and John T. Dunlop, Labor and the American Community (New York: Simon and Schuster, 1970), p. 327.

15. Dupont and Tobin, op. cit., p. 720.

16. Anderson, "School Policy and Collective Bargaining," op. cit., p. 5.

17. Ibid., p. 5.

18. Wollett, op. cit., p. 181.

19. Ibid.

20. Joel Seidman, "State Legislation in Collective Bargaining by Public Employees," Labor Law Journal 22 (January 1971): 16.

21. Cited in Lefkowitz, op. cit., p. 629.
consin Law Review, 1973, p. 999.

22. Cited in Arvid Anderson, "The Impact of Public Sector Bargaining: An Essay Dedicated to Nathan P. Fensinger," reprint, Wisconsin Law Review, 1973, p. 999.

23. Cited in Harry H. Wellington and Ralph K. Winter, Jr., "Structuring Collective Bargaining in Public Employment," Yale Law Journal 79 (April 1970): 868.

24. "An Act Relative to Collective Bargaining by Public Employees," Chapter 1018, Section 6, The Commonwealth of Massachusetts, November 26, 1973.

25. Grant F. Shipley, "Determining the Scope of Bargaining under the Indiana Education Employment Relations Act," Indiana Law Journal 49 (Spring 1974): 461-62.

26. Ibid.

27. Robert H. Chanin, "Negotiations in Public Education: Developing a Legislative Framework" (Washington, D.C.: National Education Association, 1969), p. 21.

28. Charles Miller, "What Is Negotiable?" Changing Education, Fall 1973, p. 27.

29. Albert Shanker, "The Future of Teacher Involvement in Educational Decision Making," in The Collective Dilemma: Negotiations in Education, edited by Patrick W. Carlton and Harold I. Goodwin (Worthington, Ohio: Charles Jones Publishing Co., 1969), p. 79.

30. Wollett, op. cit., pp. 177-78.

31. See "Scope of Bargaining and Management Rights," Chapter 5 in Collective Bargaining in Public Employment and the Merit System (Washington, D.C.: U.S. Department of Labor, 1971).

32. Kurt L. Hanslowe and Walter E. Oberer, "Determining the Scope of Negotiations under Public Employment Relations Statutes," Industrial and Labor Relations Review 24 (April 1971): 441.

33. Ibid., p. 440.

34. Ibid., p. 441.

35. Anderson, "School Policy and Collective Bargaining," op. cit., p. 11.

36. Cited ibid.

37. Mrs. Lloyd Herdle et al., West Irondequoit Board of Education versus West Irondequoit Teachers Association, (Albany: State of New York Public Employment Relations Board, 1971), p. 3727.

38. Ibid., p. 3728.

39. West Irondequoit Teachers Association et al., vs. Robert D. Helsby et al., Public Employment Relations Board Court Decisions, July 1974.

40. Anderson, "Teacher Collective Bargaining: Who Runs the Schools?" Fordham Urban Law Journal 2 (1973-74): 553.

41. Cited in Anderson, "School Policy and Collective Bargaining," op. cit., pp. 11-12.

42. Ibid., p. 12.

43. Yorktown Faculty Association versus Yorktown Central School District No. 2, (Albany: State of New York Public Employment Relations Board, 1974), p. 2.

44. Ibid., p. 4.

45. Letter by Charles W. Cheng to State of New York Public Employment Relations Board, May 13, 1974.

46. Jerome Lefkowitz, letter to Charles W. Cheng, November 12, 1974.

47. Anderson, "Teacher Collective Bargaining—Who Runs the Schools?" Fordham Urban Law Journal 2 (1973-74): 521.

48. Matter of Board of Higher Education of the City of New York and Professional Staff Congress (Albany: State of New York Public Employment Relations Board, April 29, 1974), pp. 3042-49.

49. Government Employee Relations Reports (Washington, D.C.: Bureau of National Affairs, July 8, 1974), pp. B7-B8.

50. National Education Association, Negotiation Research Digest (Washington, D.C.: the NEA, 1974), p. 8.

51. Anderson, op. cit., pp. 5-6.

52. Ibid., p. 6.

53. Government Employee Relations Reports (Washington, D.C.: Bureau of National Affairs, November 25, 1974), p. B-7.

54. Harry T. Edwards, "The Emerging Duty to Bargain in the Public Sector," Michigan Law Review 71 (April 1973): 921.

55. Anderson, "Teacher Collective Bargaining—Who Runs the Schools?" op. cit., p. 524.

3

THE SCOPE OF NEGOTIATIONS: CONTRACT PROVISIONS AND ADDITIONAL COMMENTARY

The Board and the Union declare their intent to cooperate in their common aims to achieve educational excellence in the Newark school system, and in the achievement of that objective recognize the fundamental necessities of the children and the legitimate expectations of the community. *

EDUCATIONAL POLICY AND BARGAINING AGREEMENTS: TEACHER POWER ?†

Once a teacher union becomes recognized as the officially

---

*Newark Contract, Declaration of Intent, <u>Agreement between the Board of Education of the City of Newark and the Newark Teachers Union</u>, p. 2.

†The review that I have undertaken in this section of four selected urban contracts was chiefly done for two reasons: (1) teachers unions have become a central force in most urban areas, outside the South, and (2) urban areas have seen increased demands on the part of community groups, particularly black groups, to participate in educational decision making. No examination will be made of states covered by meet-and-confer legislation as opposed to full bargaining statutes. Thus, California is most notably absent. For an insightful article contrasting the participation of unions in policy making in New York and California, see "Teacher Collective Bargaining—Who Runs the Schools?" <u>Fordham Urban Law Journal</u> 2 (1973-74): 505-60.

designated bargaining agent for all teachers, the next step to be taken
by the union in order to secure a measure of influence in the operations
of the schools is to negotiate an agreement that spells out the working
relationship between employer and employee. Both the content of these
agreements and the process by which the agreement is arrived at have
become subjects of widespread debate. Many observers argue that the
advent of bargaining has resulted in a situation in which teachers unions
now <u>control</u> the running of schools. Mario Fantini asserts that school
political battles have led to the "emergence of the collective teacher
as the most powerful agent in the school."[1] In the last round of negotiations in New York City, David S. Seeley, Director of the Public Education Association, issued a statement urging both the board of education and the UFT to "reject as unworkable and impractical the propo-
sition that they can reasonably and responsibly negotiate complex educational issues under the gun this summer."[2] Seeley's remarks imply
that such complex educational issues have been wrongfully included in
past bargaining contracts between the UFT and the board; this view is
shared by many community groups around the country.

At the start of negotiations in Washington, D.C., in 1974 for
instance, the District of Columbia Citizens for Better Public Education issued a series of statements concerning the exclusion of parents
from the negotiating process. The District of Columbia citizens were
expressly concerned with educational policy questions appearing in previously negotiated agreements between the Washington Teachers Union
(WTU) and the District of Columbia Board of Education.[3] In Detroit,
to head off parent-community protests, the school administration finally recommended to the Detroit Board of Education that when negotiations commenced on the new contract in June 1974, the board's negotiating team should set up a mechanism to inform community residents
periodically of what was taking place at the bargaining table.[4] Other
similar activities of community groups are considered in Chapter 5.

It is necessary to examine the contractual language of the agreements in question to see what has aroused the citizen groups.

Washington, D.C.

One area of notable controversy in negotiations is that of quality
education. In Washington, D. C., this was treated in the 1971-74
contract under the headings of curriculum development, staff development, and textbook and related educational matters.* From the

---

*For a general discussion of the rise to power of the WTU, see
Charles W. Cheng, "The Future of Collective Bargaining in Public

introduction to the article it is clear who holds power in determining these educational policies:

> The Board and the Union agree that matters dealing with quality education decisions are the Board's responsibility. The parties agree that teachers must participate in various stages of staff and curriculum development. Vital to the success of quality education is the involvement of teachers in the development and implementation of such programs. [5]

The final section of this provision outlines the structure of teacher participation as follows:

> Immediately after this Agreement goes into effect, a joint Board-union committee will be established. This committee shall meet at least once a month with the Division of Instructional Services for the purpose of reviewing the actions taken to implement this Article and to determine jointly what additional actions shall be taken. The first such meeting shall take place not less than 30 days after this Agreement goes into effect. [6]

Hence, the board maintains control over these educational policies, on the one hand, while on the other, the union has secured codetermination in the formulation of what "additional actions" are to be taken in the respective areas. Theoretically this clause can serve to promote a cooperative relationship between the administration and the union, and the language would also permit a union veto over contemplated actions. Nevertheless, the union has in no way obtained complete control over these significant educational policy questions, as will be seen in the contract provisions under review. * Also, there is no process for community input and/or participation in the day-to-day implementation of the important contractual provision quoted above.

Schools: A Case Study of the Washington Teacher's Union," master's thesis, Antioch Graduate School of Education, July 25, 1972.

*I was a chief negotiator for the first three collective bargaining agreements between the Washington Teachers Union and the Washington, D.C., Board of Education (1967-72). With respect to major educational policy decisions, the last contract that was negotiated, which is the one now in effect, saw our organization actually lose a contractual decision-making voice in the vital area of curriculum and staff development.

Another common contractual clause that is of deep concern to parents relates to pupil discipline. In part, the Washington, D.C., contract calls for the following procedure:

A. The Board and the Union recognize that a good discipline program is understood to foster a warm accepting school and classroom atmosphere whereby children develop self-control and self-direction, and that the maintenance of discipline is necessary in order that an effective educational program may be conducted. To achieve this end, both parties recognize that actions taken to resolve student difficulties should be profitable and acceptable learning situations.

B. A teacher shall be free to send for the Principal or his designee to escort, or to send or escort, to the Principal's office any pupil who conducts himself in such a manner that learning for himself and other children in the classroom is seriously handicapped, or if the safety of himself, other pupils, or the teacher is seriously threatened. [7]

On the critical question of who decides when an excluded student is returned to class, the contract does specify a form of due process; however, once the procedure is followed, the administration ultimately makes the final determination.

C. When a student is excluded from class, the teacher will confer with the Principal or his designee, to provide the necessary information concerning the problem and shall provide a written statement of the problem within 24 hours.

D. Before the student is returned to a classroom, there shall be a conference arranged by the Principal or his designee, which shall include but not be limited to the teacher, the student, the parent to guardian, if available, and the Principal or his designee. Any decision reached shall be made with the best interest of the student or students in mind. The teacher shall have the right to be accompanied by a representative of his choice in all phases of follow-up procedures following the removal of a pupil from a classroom at the teacher's request. [8]

Another standard negotiating article, appropriately titled Meeting on Policy Matters, has to do with regular meetings between the union and the school administration.

> The Union and Board representatives shall hold meetings
> at least once a month unless cancelled by mutual agree-
> ment to discuss school policies and problems relating to
> the implementation of the Agreement. Any agreement
> reached on the interpretation of any part of the Agree-
> ment shall be reduced to writing and signed by the Board
> or its designee and the Union. It shall become an adden-
> dum to this Agreement. [9]

Technically, the language if strictly adhered to simply involves implementation and interpretation; yet in practice these meetings can result
in the negotiation of issues not necessarily found in the agreement.
This can provide the central union staff with direct access to policy
making, but it should be borne in mind that it does not guarantee access.

A related common clause that has caused concern to parents
deals with Matters Not Covered, as follows:

> The parties agree that by mutual consent they will con-
> sult and negotiate on matters not covered by this Agree-
> ment which are proper subjects for collective bargain-
> ing. [10]

Of course, in this provision the key phrase is "mutual consent," but
nonetheless there is an opening for union access.

Finally, one of the more controversial policy and working conditions provisions found in nearly every bargaining agreement has to do
with class size. Like most agreements, the Washington, D.C. agreement does place limits on class size, but the conditions under which
the negotiated class size can be exceeded tend to undermine the widely-
held view that the unions control class size. This is not to say that
grievances will not be filed by individual teachers when class size is
higher than specified in the contract, but only that in Washington, as
well as in other cities, if an "acceptable reason" for altering class
size exists, the grievance will be denied. *

---

*The Washington class size provision reads as follows:

a. Except as provided in "b" below, maximum class size
   shall not exceed the following:
   1. 15 for pre-kindergarten (non-compulsory)
   2. 20 for kindergarten through grade 2
   3. 25 for grades 3 through 6
   4. 25 for secondary academic classes

Newark

Although not to be compared to the Ocean Hill-Brownsville strike, the Newark Teachers Union strike of 1971 was one of the most bitter conflicts between organized teachers and the community. In light of the intense politcal struggle waged by the union in the 1971-72 strike, it is important to see what the resulting Newark contract contains.

The curriculum clause calls for the "direct participation" of the union in curriculum revision and educational improvement, as follows:

ARTICLE XXIII—CURRICULUM REVISION

To serve the needs of Newark's students in a changing society, curriculum revision and educational improve- ment on all levels from early childhood through high school must be a constant ongoing process in the schools in Newark. In order to involve the direct participation of the Newark Teacher's Union, as the collective negoti- ation representative of teachers and other instructional employees, in the process, the Board agrees that the Union may nominate a representative for inclusion on all

------

5. 12 for remedial classes
6. 8 for retarded and emotionally disturbed, sight con- servation, or hearing classes
7. 18 for industrial arts and home economics classes
8. 18 for shops in vocational high schools

b. An acceptable reason for altering the class size may be any of the following:
1. Lack of sufficient funds for equipment, supplies, or rental of classroom space;
2. there is no classroom space and/or personnel avail- able to permit scheduling of any additional class or classes in order to reduce class size;
3. conformity to the class size objective would result in the organization of half or part-time classes;
4. a class larger than the above is necessary and de- sirable in order to provide for specialized or experi- mental instruction;
5. a class larger than the maximum is necessary for placement of pupils in a subject for a class of which there is only one on a grade level;
6. size of specific classroom space is inadequate.

presently ongoing curriculum committees, and on any to
be established in the future during the period of this agreement.

In addition, there shall be a conference conducted each
December and April between a representative committee
of no more than five (5) individuals representing the Newark Teacher's Union with the Assistant Superintendent
in charge of Curriculum Services and any immediate
staff members of the Assistant Superintendent. The purpose of this conference will be to afford the NTU an opportunity of presenting to the Department of Curriculum
Services its concernc and views with respect to any overall curricular activities within the Newark Public School
System. [11]

Under this provision the union has gained an important entry into
policy making, but neither control, nor for that matter joint decision
making, has been achieved. Very interestingly, under a related provision entitled "Cultural Pluralism," the parties have made a strong
commitment to establish bilingual or multilingual programs—a policy
area taking on more importance and controversy in a number of central urban cities today; this provision reads as follows:

ARTICLE IX—CULTURAL PLURALISM

A. The Board shall include in its calendar reference to
   specific commemorative dates in AfroAmerican, Puerto Rican history, as well as other dates rcflccting such
   dates [sic] among national and cultural groups typical
   of the population of Newark.
B. The Board shall recruit teachers who are bilingual or
   multilingual to scrve in establishing special classes
   for non-English speaking students where needed, and
   the Board shall continue to maintain its policy of making classes available to all students in need of such
   classes. [12]

The Newark contract does not contain a pupil discipline article.
According to the union president, Carol Graves, the existing rules of
the board make such a provision unnecessary.

As in Washington, Newark has a provision calling for regular
meetings on matters of broad policy between the union and the board,
as follows:

Section 8—Board-Union Conferences

Meetings shall be scheduled between the Board and the
Union to discuss matters of mutual concern in terms
of educational policy, the implementation of this Agreement, and any other topics consistent with the objectives
stated in the Declaration of Intent of this Agreement. No
more than five (5) such meetings may be required in any
school year by either party to this Agreement, but additional meetings may be held by agreement between the
Union and the Board.
At least five (5) school days prior to the holding of each
such meeting, the Union will meet with the Superintendent
to review with him the topics to be discussed. In the event
that law or existing Board policy places one or more of
the topics to be discussed under the discretionary jurisdiction and prerogative of the Superintendent, the Superintendent may undertake, in cooperation with the Union,
to dispose of questions raised with reference thereto
without waiting for further action by the Board. [13]

The Declaration of Intent referred to in the above section is as follows:

the Board and the Union declare their intent to cooperate
in their common aims to achieve educational excellence
in the Newark school system, and in the achievement of
that objective recognize the fundamental necessities of
the children and the legitimate expectations of the community. [14]

Taken together, the two clauses attempt to balance the interest of the
community and the students with that of the union. Union access to
policy making is plainly evident.
    The Matters Not Covered section in this agreement also under-
scores the fact that in many policy areas negotiations with the union
must occur before any new actions can be taken.

ARTICLE XXIV—MATTERS NOT COVERED

Section 2

The Board agrees that it will make no change in existing
Board policy or practice related to employee wages,
hours, and conditions of employment and not specifically
covered by this Agreement without prior negotiation with
the Union. [15]

Finally, Newark's contract contains a clause dealing with account-ability, a subject that has aroused widespread community concern a-cross the nation. Such a clause does not appear in the Washington agreement. Importantly, this clause provides for inclusion of other citizen groups in its implementation.

ARTICLE XIX—ACCOUNTABILITY STUDY

The Board and the Union agree to set up a Committee on account-ability to consist of:
A. Five individuals appointed by the NTU.
B. Five individuals appointed by the Board.
C. Five individuals representing:
    a. Parents (one to be selected by the PTA's and Title 1 Advisory Groups).
    b. Student (one to be selected by the Newark Stu-dent Federation).
    c. Organized labor (one to be selected by the AFL-CIO of Essex County).
    d. Business (one to be selected by the Chamber of Commerce).
    e. Mayor's Education Task Force (one to be select-ed by that body).
Each of the groups named above shall be invited to submit a name for inclusion on the committee which shall be ac-ceptable both to the Union and the Board representatives on the Committee on Accountability.[16]

It is not made clear what will be done with the results of the study, however.

The full committee shall begin to operate as rapidly as feasible and shall present a first report of its findings and recommendations during the month of July, 1973, to the Board and the Union.[17]

With respect to class size, the opening paragraph and the "ex-ceptions" clause point out that, while the board agrees with the union on specific limitations on class size, this matter is not controlled by the union. The pertinent sections read as follows:

Section 5—Class Size

It is recognized by this Agreement that the Board and Administration have worked to reduce class size in

every school to reach a class size which is most suitable
to the level or area of instruction involved. It is further
recognized that until the present building program is
completed, it will be extremely difficult to attain optimal
class sizes. The agreements on class size contained below are, therefore, temporary and in no way represent
anything other than a short-range effort to improve on
the present situation.

. . .

J. Exceptions. An acceptable justification for exceeding
   the maximum class size limitations listed above may
   be any one or more of the following.
   1. There is no more classroom space available in the
   building which will permit scheduling any additional
   classes in order to reduce class size, and other school
   facilities which meet approved standards and are not
   unreasonably inconvenient or not (sic) available.
   2. In order to achieve the prescribed class size it
   would be necessary to schedule one or more part-
   time classes in either elementary or special schools.
   3. The Union and administration agree that a class
   larger than the prescribed maximum is desirable for
   purposes of experiment with large-group instruction.
   (The conditions of employment in such cases shall be
   negotiated.)
   4. Team-teaching arrangements are in use which operate under a teacher with the assistance of either additional teachers, teacher-interns, teacher aides or any
   combination of them.
   5. Additional students are added to the school enrollment after March 1.[18]

   The Accountability and Cultural Pluralism provisions in the
Newark contract point out two steps that can be taken to deal with community concerns in the bilateral process. However, in Newark these
steps were taken only after great strife among the union, the board,
and the community.

Detroit

   The major portion of the Detroit Federation of Teachers (DFT)
involvement in curriculum appears in the section called Quality Integrated Education, by which it would appear that the union has obtained

a measure of joint decision making in this area. In part the curriculum article calls for the following types of cooperation (emphasis added):

III. QUALITY INTEGRATED EDUCATION

In order to assure positive action designed to implement the commitments expressed in the Preamble of this Agreement and in furtherance of past recommendations and action of the Board, Union, Administration, professional staff, and various concerned citizen groups, the Union and the Administration will continue and will accelerate their efforts to provide quality integrated education in the following manner:

A. Textbook and Curriculum Improvement

1. In order to meet the real and vital learning needs of children in this multi-religious, multi-ethnic society in which we live, textbooks and other curriculum material for each pupil in all classes shall be used pursuant to the guidelines established by the Board and outlined in 1968 Textbook Report, Publication 1-112, or its successor, prepared by the Intergroup Relations Department of the Division of School-Community Relations.

2. Use of textbooks and other curriculum material for each pupil in all American history classes in order to cover in depth the contribution of Negro and other minority groups in each unit taught, and inclusion of such material as part of the course of study in Curriculum Guides.

3. Use of supplemental reading materials dealing with Negro and other minority group contributions, e.g. Jews, Chinese, and American Indians.

4. Use of comprehensive units in world history which cover African, Asian and Latin-American history at appropriate grade levels.

5. Use of available Federal funds from the Elementary-Secondary Education Act to reduce the class size in inner city schools to maximum of 25 students in regular grades with proportional reduction in Special Education classes and classes on half-day sessions.

6. Increased use of special services in inner city schools, including psychological, medical, and dental services, through Federally funded programs and/or by taking fullest advantage of available community resources.

> 7. The Board shall designate personnel necessary to
> assure the implementation of the above sections.
> 8. The TV series "Americans from Africa" shall con-
> tinue with appropriate modifications and teachers shall
> be encouraged to utilize the program. [19]

This same article calls for staff and pupil integration, a joint
union-board committee to work with universities in developing a required course of study "geared toward understanding and working with
children with cultural differences," and the elimination of culturally
biased tests. [20]

The Detroit contract outlines a relatively detailed procedure for
joint meetings on policy matters.

> A. The Board, through its designated representatives,
>   shall meet regularly, not less than monthly, with the
>   Union, through its designated representatives, for
>   the purpose of discussing school policies and problems
>   relating to the implementation of this Agreement.
>   In the event the Superintendent, or his designated rep-
>   resentative, and the Union are unable to resolve their
>   differences on any policy matter, they shall present
>   separate written or oral reports to the Personnel Com-
>   mittee of the Board of Education, which reports shall
>   contain the points of agreement and disagreement. A
>   Conference Committee composed of the Superintendent,
>   Union representatives (selected by the Union) shall be
>   established for the purpose of reaching an understand-
>   ing and agreement.
>   The Conference Committee shall submit a written re-
>   port to the full Board of Education, which report shall
>   set forth any agreements reached by the Conference
>   Committee or, in the absence of agreement, shall
>   state the respective positions of the parties and the
>   specific issues which the Conference Committee has
>   failed to resolve. This written report shall be re-
>   ceived at the next regular meeting of the Board of Edu-
>   cation immediately following the last meeting of the
>   Conference Committee, or at a special meeting of
>   the Board of Education publicly called for such pur-
>   pose. [21]

Parts of the above provision point to the possibility of reaching
a negotiated agreement, thus assuring the union access to policy

making. Nevertheless, the final section seems to indicate that the board will make the final determination.

Detroit's contract contains an extremely lengthy discipline procedure, which will only partly be included here. From an examination of the article, it is clear that the DFT has secured a provision which provides teachers a high degree of influence in this policy area. The most pertinent passages are as follows:

VIII. DISCIPLINE

A. Within the framework of the Discipline and Corporal Punishment Policy of the Board of Education, a consistent and reasonable discipline procedure shall be worked out within each unit by the school principal, assistant principal, department heads, counselors and classroom teachers.

B. The Teacher's authority in his classroom is undermined when pupils discover that he has little or no administrative backing in discipline. As a result the entire school suffers deterioration in standards, morale, and climate favorable for teaching and learning.

C. A teacher may exclude from his class a child who in the teacher's opinion is causing serious disruption. The teacher should confer with the principal or assistant principal or counselor to provide the necessary information concerning the problem and shall provide a statement of the problem in writing at the time or within twenty-four hours. The teacher will re-admit the child after some adjustment has been made, following a conference with the child at least two of the following parties: an administrator, a counselor, school social worker, school psychologist, attendance officer, a parent of the child.
The teacher shall be present unless he feels that his presence is not necessary. The teacher shall be informed as to the results of the conference and/or the adjustment.

D. Following such a conference one of several courses of action will be taken.
1. The child will be returned to the class with the understanding that he will correct the behavior.
2. Depending upon the seriousness of the infraction, the child may be returned to class while his case is being referred to one of the special services by the school

social worker, school psychologist, or an attendance
officer.

3. In case all the teachers who work with a child in
regular classes recommend suspension and the principal disagrees, the teachers shall address a request
to the region superintendent who shall meet with the
principal and the teachers to determine if the child
shall be suspended.

4. The child will be suspended by the principal. [22]

Further, the article calls for action to be taken against a principal for failing to support teachers in the maintenance of discipline, as
follows:

J. Where a principal is unwilling or unable to support
teachers in maintaining school discipline, the principal's superior shall counsel with him and in the event
his performance is not improved further appropriate
action shall be taken. [23]

Moreover, in the very controversial area of corporal punishment,
an issue often protested by the black community, the contract permits
physical punishment within certain restraints:

M. It is recognized that, in developing responsible student
conduct the positive disciplinary techniques of example,
counseling, and guidance should take precedence over
punitive disciplinary measures. In this regard, this
Agreement provides for communication with parents
on matters of discipline, safety, and other local school
regulations (Article XI, Section C), and, Union-spon-
sered workshops on classroom management (Article
XVII, Section G, fifth paragraph).

It is general policy to expect that teachers will maintain discipline by means other than the use of corporal
punishment as a routine measure is not contemplated.
(sic) This policy does not prohibit corporal punishment
(as provided by Chapter 15, School Code of 1955, Section 755, et. seq.) but does restrict its use to those
cases in which there is no adequate substitute treat-
ment. However, a distincttion must be made between
physical restraint, which is occasionally necessary
to keep a young person from injuring himself or others,
and punishment, which is utilized to discourage repe-
tition of misbehavior. . . .

> Teachers will receive full support of the principal and
> the central administration in actions taken by them
> pertaining to discipline, provided thay act in accord
> with the provisions of this Article. This support shall
> include defense of the teacher's action by the princi-
> pal against complaints of parents as well as legal
> assistance by the central administration in the event
> that a criminal complaint is made or civil court action
> is instituted for damages. [24]

   With firm contractual language of this kind, it is not difficult to
discern why parents and community people would be vitally interested
in participating in the formulation of such policies. Indeed, Harry H.
Wellington and Ralph K. Winter, Jr., single out discipline as one of
the policy areas that should be eliminated from the bargaining because
other groups have an immediate interest in it.
   Detroit's class-size provision presents a similar pattern to
those of Newark and Washington. Notably, in the establishment of a
class-size review committee, the union has only gained the power to
recommend. However, the special conference called for in case no
resolution is forthcoming could result in a negotiated settlement. The
relevant provision reads as follows:

B. Class Size Review Board

> In an effort to effectively implement innovative ap-
> proaches to the complex class size problems in the
> Detroit Public Schools a Class Size Review Board
> has been established for the purpose of hearing com-
> plaints filed by any teacher whose class exceeds 36,
> or by any teacher who alleges that a class size above
> 35 is the result of inequitable school organization.
> This board shall be composed of at least three teach-
> ers selected by the Union and at least three adminis-
> trators appointed by the Superintendent.
> The Class Size Review Board shall have the power to
> investigate any complaints received; to select particu-
> lar schools and particular classes in selected schools
> for review; to effectively recommend the priority and
> method of correcting any inequities found and the power
> to recommend the use of specific State and/or Federal
> funds. Any recommendation of the Class Size Review
> Board which is not acted upon within thirty days from
> date of said recommendation, shall be the subject of a
> special meeting of the conference committee of the
> Board of Education and the Union. [25]

Two provisions appear in Detroit's agreement that are not covered in the two previously discussed contracts. Because of their specific reference to community participation, they are worth citing. The
Parent-Teacher Conference article contains a clause that clearly
points to past and perhaps anticipated conflicts between parents and
teachers. * In part the Article states the following:

> The Union fully supports community and especially paren-
> tal participation in the school program. However, such
> participation must not be allowed to distract pupils at
> work in the classroom(s), or in any way disrupt or ob-
> struct the school's instructional program. This would
> make the community's interest in the second operation
> self-defeating. [26]

The other provision speaks directly to the question of decentralization. Detroit operates a decentralized school district as a result
of a state law that grew out of the demands for community control of
schools by a number of black groups. This clause leaves no doubt
that the union and the central board will continue to negotiate the overall bargaining agreement.

C. Community-School

> An advisory committee of administrators, counselors,
> teachers (selected by the Union) and community repre-
> sentatives may be organized at the local school level
> for the purpose of assuring greater communication
> with parents on matters of discipline, safety, and other
> local school regulations. Such committees are encour-
> aged to coordinate efforts within their high school con-
> stellation and with schools in other constellations.
> Plans developed by these committees shall not include
> any matter which is inconsistent with the collective
> bargaining Agreement, other Board of Education pol-
> icy, and/or the policies of other public agencies. [27]

---

*Washington's contract does contain a clause dealing with parent/
teacher conferences, but although there is no language found in Washington that is similar to that of Detroit, the Washington clause has been
a bone of contention between the PTAs and the WTU because of the
clause that frees teachers from the responsibility of attending the business meetings of the PTA. Many parents believe teachers should be
obligated to attend.

As Joseph Cronin observed in The Control of Urban Schools, one of the reasons the decentralization bill passed the Michigan legislature was "legislative guarantee of teacher seniority rights, tenure, and the rights of unions to bargain with the central board, along with retention of existing benefits."[28]

A Matters Not Covered section does not appear in this contract. It may be that the meeting on policies is comprehensive enough to sufficiently guarantee the union continuous access to policy making on a regular basis.

New York City*

When Alan Rosenthal did his study, Pedagogues and Power: Teacher Groups in School Politics, he concluded that the UFT had gained more access to policy making than any of the other four organizations he studied.[29] A number of observers, among them Mario Fantini; the Public Education Association of New York City; and numerous community groups, particularly in black and Puerto Rican communities, contend that the UFT has obtained supreme control over the running of the city schools. Certainly the fact that the union was able to crush the Ocean Hill-Brownsville experimental school district in 1968-69 demonstrates the decisive power of the New York local. The contract itself was the lengthiest of the four reviewed here, covering a broad range of subjects in over 100 pages; yet surprisingly, the contract language in the policy areas looked at does not necessarily reveal complete control by the UFT. For instance, notably absent was a comprehensive provision dealing with curriculum matters, similar to those found in the other three contracts. There is an important provision that alludes to curriculum called Experimentation:

ARTICLE XIV

The Board of Education and the Union recognize that a sound educational program requires not only the efficient use of existing resources but also constant experimentation with new methods and organization. The Union agrees that experimentation presupposes flexibility in assigning

---

*For a comprehensive analysis contrasting the Detroit and New York contracts see Etta Miller, An Analysis of Two Teacher Union Contracts with Large Urban School Systems (New York: Center for Urban Education, ERIC Document reproduction ED 088-239, 1969).

and programming pedagogical and other professional personnel. Hence, the Union will facilitate its members'
voluntary participation in new ventures that may depart
from usual procedures. The Board agrees that educational experimentation will be consistent with the standards of working conditions prescribed in this agreement. [30]

Clearly, the language discloses the crucial influence the union
has in this broad arena. In practice, nearly any new curriculum matter, staff training, new program, or related matter would seemingly
come under this rubric: experimentation. Again, it is provisions of
this kind that often spark community concern; for example, with increasing demand for bilingual-multicultural programming and staffing,
the union appears to be strongly influencing the decision about exactly
what the characteristics of such a program should be, and perhaps
whether there should be such a program at all. Thus the union's evident power of veto provides enough authority to make a contractual provision dealing with serious policy matters virtually unnecessary.

New York's discipline clause is short:

ARTICLE XV
PROCEDURES FOR HANDLING SPECIAL BEHAVIOR
    PROBLEMS

The Board agrees that the procedures and policies concerning the problem of disruptive children, embodied
in the Special Circular which is reproduced in the pages
following this agreement, except that, after the first
year of this agreement, the Chancellor may modify the
circular in accordance with such recommendations of
the Chancellor's Committee on Disruptive Children as
the Chancellor proposes to the Union and the Union finds
acceptable.
The provisions of the circular shall be subject to the
grievance procedure and to arbitration only for the purpose of determining whether there has been a failure to
comply with the procedural steps prescribed in the circular. [31]

It should be recalled that in the 1967 negotiations the union's
insistence on a strong removal clause to deal with what it termed
"disruptive students" aroused widespread resentment and anger among
a large number of black and Puerto Rican people. This issue sharpened

the racial polarization in New York City's school system a year before
the Ocean Hill-Brownsville strike. * Article 15 is a compromise. The
union did not win the absolute right for teachers to remove students—
which was the essence of the union demand—but the provision reveals
that the union is very much a part of decision making in this policy area.

The class-size provision is similar to the others; in fact, the
UFT approach to class size has become the model for most AFT locals.
There are specified maximums for prekindergarten through high school,
which are subject to the standard exceptions clause:

> An acceptable reason for exceeding the maximum class
> size limitations listed above may be any of the following:
> 1) There is no space available to permit scheduling of any
>   additional class or classes in order to reduce class
>   size.
> 2) Conformity to the class size objective would result in
>   placing additional classes on short time schedules.
> 3) Conformity to the class size objective would result in
>   the organization of half-classes.
> 4) A class larger than the maximum is necessary or de-
>   sirable in order to provide for specialized or experi-
>   mental instruction, or for IGC instruction, or for
>   placement of pupils in a subject class of which there
>   is only one in a grade.
> In the event that it is necessary to assign a teacher to a
> class which exceeds the maximum size listed above, the
> principal shall stipulate the reason in writing to the teach-
> er and to the Chancellor. Such statement of reasons may
> be available for examination by the Union in the office of
> the Chancellor. [32]

The UFT provision dealing with joint meetings on policy matters
indicates that legally all that is required is consultation:

> The Chancellor or his designee representative shall meet
> and consult once a month during the school year with rep-
> resentatives of the United Federation of Teachers on mat-
> ters of mutual concern.

---

*A good account of this issue and how it was eventually settled
can be found in Ida Klaus, "The Evolution of a Collective Bargaining
Relationship in Public Education: New York City's Changing Seven-
Year History," Michigan Law Review 67 (March 1969): 1033-66.

The head of the school and the school chapter committee
shall meet once a month during the school year to con-
sult on matters of school policy and on questions relating to the implementations of this agreement. [33]

Although monthly meetings are required, as in the other agreements, there is no indication of obligatory joint decision making in the
general area of interim policy making.

While the clause covering policy meetings would appear weak
(weak in the sense the Union has neither obtained joint and/or decisive
influence in formulating policy), the Matters Not Covered section is
much stronger, since negotiations are mandatory and the mutual consent of the parties is not required.

ARTICLE XII
MATTERS NOT COVERED

With respect to matters not covered by this agreement
which are proper subjects for collective baragining, the
Board agrees that it will make no changes without appropriate prior consultation and negotiation with the Union.
The Board will continue its present policy with respect
to sick leave, sabbatical leaves, vacations and holidays
except insofar as change is commanded by law.
All existing determination, authorizations, by-laws, regulations, rules, rulings, resolutions, certifications, or-
ders, directives, and other actions, made, issued or entered into by the Board of Education governing or affecting salary and working conditions of the employees in the
bargaining unit shall continue in force during the term of
this agreement, except insofar as change is commanded
by law. [34]

Not surprisingly, given the severe conflict and the clash over
community control in New York City, the UFT contract contains an
extremely detailed provision covering what amounts to a teacher's
complaint article regarding community and student harassment. The
section is called Special Complaints. Regardless of what views one
might have held concerning the Ocean Hill-Brownsville struggle, the
fact remains that upon a careful reading of this clause, it is at least
understandable why some black and Puerto Rican communities were
profoundly concerned about being excluded from the decision-making
process that led to this agreement. The article lays out its purpose
as follows:

ARTICLE XVI
SPECIAL COMPLAINTS

It is the declared objective of the parties to encourage
the prompt and informal resolution of special complaints
not covered by the grievance procedure and to dispose of
such complaints as they arise and to provide recourse to
orderly procedures for their adjustment.
A. Definition
A "special complaint" is a complaint by an employee in
the bargaining unit that persons or groups are engaging
in a course of harassing conduct, or in acts of intimidation, which are being directed against him in the course
of his employment and that the school principal or community or assistant superintendent has not afforded the
employee adequate relief against such recourse of conduct or acts of intimidation. [35]

While the article provides for an elaborate but speedy process
for resolving such disputes, including the use of third-party neutrals,
final determination is made by the board. The utility of such a procedure for resolving conflicts can be seen, but at the same time it must
be noted that no such mechanisms are available to poor, black and
Puerto Rican parents who have "special complaints" regarding teachers
or the union. The office of an ombudsman is used for such a purpose,
in many cities to allow all parties having grievances to petition for
remedies.

INCREASED TEACHER POWER (BUT HOW MUCH?)

A review of these selected contract provisions reveals that a
wide number of policy issues are included in the final negotiated agreements. Indisputably, teachers unions have managed to become involved
in the formulation of a variety of significant educational policy questions, but this participation, as spelled out contractually, does not
necessarily disclose union control over the areas cited here. In a
1973-74 survey dealing with the question of teacher union influence in
critical policy areas, the Fordham Urban Law Journal, after examining a number of bargaining agreements in New York and similar arrangements in California, reached this conclusion:

Finally, no significant dimunition of the local school
board's control over the formulation of educational

policy was observed in this study. The most significant
intrusion of teachers in this area were agreements and
contracts establishing a system of formal advice and
consultation. While one might argue that the board's
control over educational policy is diminished when it's
compelled to agree to an advisory committee structure,
the fact remains that the ultimate power of decision is
retained by the school boards in both states. [36]

This finding is not without significance. Certainly, the contracts
reviewed would tend to fit the conclusion reached in the Fordham
study. * There are, however, a few notable exceptions. There were
certain areas in which joint decision making was obtained, thereby reducing the absolute control previously held by the board of education
in those matters. Joint decision remains the most substantive power
achieved by the teacher unions;† but nevertheless, there were no areas
considered where the union appeared to have secured ultimate control
over the operations of the school. The unions in these cities have
emerged as a powerful force within the last ten years. Their impact

---

*In a 1970 study, Charles R. Perry and Wesley A. Wildman,
after analyzing a number of teacher bargaining agreements, reached
the same conclusion as the Fordham study. As they put it, "While
myriad 'policy' and 'professional' subjects have received attention in
school bargaining, collective negotiations has not yet resulted in any
wholesale restructuring of the traditional control patterns affecting
basic school district policy or its implementation." The Impact of Negotiations in Public Education: The Evidence from the Schools, (Worthington, Ohio: Charles A. Jones Publishing Co., 1970), p. 188. And in
their study of over 300 teachers (excluding New York City) Dunn and
Bailey found that classroom teachers do not perceive that any significant gains have been made in securing teacher access to policy making.
Because of this teacher perception, they predict that in the future in
New York State more emphasis will be placed on teacher participation in educational decision making. See Frank Dunn and Thomas C.
Bailey, "Identifiable Trends in Teacher Attitudes Toward Collective
Negotiations," Journal of Collective Negotiations in the Public Sector
2 (Spring 1973): 113-24.

†Although the selection of the contract subjects reviewed here
was primarily based on expressed community interest in these topics,
this is not to suggest that there are no other subjects, now included
in teacher contracts, of equal concern to groups outside the bargaining structure.

is greater now than ever before. Even though teachers unions have not won the kind of decisive control spoken of by some, the fact that crucial policy issues are being decided in the bilateral relationship by union leaders and school administrators remains a source of concern to those troubled by a bargaining structure that excludes the poor and the other minorities who have a stake in what is negotiated.

ADDITIONAL SCHOLARLY OPINION ON SCOPE

It may be helpful at this point to review what some other observers and participants of teacher bargaining have had to say about the overall developments related to the expansion of scope and its impact on the decision-making process in education.

Parallel developments in the private sector must be noted. At a seminar on collective bargaining held at Harvard University in the fall of 1973, Robert Gorman, a visiting professor at the Harvard Law School, said there were two major issues ahead regarding conditions of employment in the private sector, these being quality of life in the work place and environmental issues emerging from the products of the work place. Of greater import is Gorman's prediction that these topics will soon become mandatory subjects for bargaining.[37] Negotiating these kinds of items will substantially broaden the scope of negotiations far beyond the items generally termed bread-and-butter issues. Recently, some United Automobile Workers (UAW) locals have sought to deal with pollution problems. A more concrete example is the Oil, Chemical and Atomic Workers Union (OCAWU) in its strike against Shell Oil. At issue was the safety and health of the workers at the work place. Also, during the last negotiations between the coal miners and the mine owners, the United Mine Workers (UMW) placed great stress on safety issues. Perhaps these positions disclose the emergence of a more vigorous attempt on the part of some private unions to seriously challenge the management prerogative doctrine. No longer can it be claimed, as Edward B. Shils and C. Taylor Whittier did in 1968, that public-sector unions are moving more swiftly and "more radically" into "an invasion of management rights than in private industry."[38] This is not the place to argue whether public employee unions had any substantial impact on other unions, as one might conclude from Shils and Whittier; indeed, one might make a case that these recent stances taken by private unions concerning the scope of negotiations are influencing some public employee unions.

In fact, Gorman said it was too early to tell how wide the scope of negotiations will be in public school bargaining. His own view, shared by many, is that because of their training and the nature of

their work, the teachers' scope of bargaining in public education is
likely to widen in the next few years. Gorman believes that if some
states pass statutes that permit a wide range of bargainable items and
the other states see that such statutes don't result in the collapse of
the school system, then in his view more states are likely to follow
suit. [39] As we have seen, state statutes are not able to resolve the
dispute. Robert D. Helsby goes so far as to say that "It is significant
that more of the recently enacted state laws approach this problem by
avoiding it rather than by attempting to deal with it in advance."[40]

We have further seen that the scope has widened. Some maintain
that the emergence of the unions as a powerful interest group enriches
the decision-making process, bringing the long-absent voice of the
teacher to educational policy making. Donald H. Wollett has best cap-
tured this notion by arguing that teachers unions have become an important and necessary countervailing political force. He puts it this way:

> The history of public education seems to indicate that
> neither school boards nor other essentially political
> agencies, standing alone, can realistically be relied
> upon to provide a meaningful domain of academic free-
> dom for public school teachers. Teachers can achieve
> this objective only through the development of strong
> local organizations which are capable of mobilizing and
> using power in appropriate ways. Such teacher organi-
> zations can give school boards caught between the needs
> of education and the pressures of public interest groups
> the courage and confidence to "opt for education."[41]

Nevertheless, there is a growing school of thought that argues that
public employee unions do pose a threat to ordered government in the
sense that they gain excessive influence in shaping public policy through
collective bargaining unless scope is restricted. Essentially this argument holds that the establishment of codetermination between unions
and management means the sharing or even surrendering of policy-
making areas to groups that have no legal responsibility to the public.
Harry H. Wellington and Ralph K. Winter, Jr., as already indicated,
have written extensively on this matter, and they stress that expansion
of the scope of bargaining beyond traditional subjects gives unions an
upper hand over other citizen groups, who must employ the political
process to gain access to decision making. [42]

In contrast to Wellington and Winter, and striking a theme somewhat similar to Wollett's countervailing force idea, Harry T. Edwards
has placed teacher power in the following perspective:

> It cannot . . . be controverted that, in theory, decisions
> on governmental priorities are properly politcal and
> should be responsive to the desires of the constituency
> as a whole rather than the values of a labor union. Yet,
> in reality, the process of resource allocation in govern-
> ment is the outcome of a tug-of-war between many orga-
> nized interest groups.[43]

Lee C. Shaw and Theodore R. Clark, Jr., on the other hand, argue for a restriction on scope and a retention of the management-rights
doctrine, and they state that this doctrine rests on the "concept that
it is management's duty to act and it is the union's duty to challenge if
the union feels that management's action is contrary to the negotiated
agreement."[44] Such a view envisions a labor relations situation in
which the union is considered a "watchdog" while management is seen
as the acting party. However, Derek C. Bok and John T. Dunlop indicate that this management-rights doctrine is becoming less and less
persuasive in efforts to settle problems with public employees.[45]

The trend in public employee bargaining seems to sustain the
view expressed by Bok and Dunlop. Despite all the commentary, it
would appear that unless the legal circumstances change, the expansion
of scope is most likely to come from the battle fought at the negotiating
table. The conclusion to an article by Wollett in the Oregon Law Review
best sums up this viewpoint:

> In the public sector, as well as the private, what is bar-
> gained about, as well as what the terms of the bargaining
> are, should be the function of the bargaining process, not
> of abstract concerns over sovereignty or responsiveness
> to misconceived legislative constraints.[46]

It is worth underscoring here that several advocates of increased
teacher decision making, such as Ralph P. Dupont and Robert D. Tobin,
strongly favor legislation guaranteeing teachers the right to participate
in the determination of educational policy;[47] yet even favorable legislation of this kind could place severe restrictions on bargaining. That
is to say, creative collective bargaining may be less likely to occur
under legislative statutes that deal with the scope of bargaining.

Perhaps this is the notion Bok and Dunlop had in mind when they
wrote: "A most significant function of collective bargaining in this
country is the continuing design and redesign of the institution itself."[48]
They then added, "The bargaining parties must reshape their bargaining arrangement from time to time in response to experience and emerging new problems."[49]

Clearly, one of these pressing new problems centers around the increasing power being achieved by teachers unions in the formulation of public policy. As Ida Klaus has written, one of the issues posed by public employee bargaining is whether "the resolution of public interest issues in serious collective bargaining clashes can in fact be guided by just and proper needs of the public and the community."[50] Hy Kornbluh, codirector of the Program for the National Study of Collective Negotiations in Education, University of Michigan, and an advocate of teacher decision making through bargaining, has summed up the issue as well as anyone, as follows:

> There will be diverse pressures on teacher organizations because the consequences of this collective bargaining overlap may come in conflict with the interests of other groups. We have to work on new decision-making structures that recognize the roles of these groups and that allow for expression of their legitimate interests.[51]

Those who are concerned with the expansion of scope and its relationship to the public interest are of course by implication raising a question regarding the representative character of the board of education itself. Theoretically, at least, the board represents the community's interest; therefore the community is participating in the negotiating process through either elected or appointed representatives. This question of the representativesness of boards of education will be taken up in the next chapter. Before doing so, one final point should be made.

A side from some of the philosophical and theoretical questions surrounding the scope of bargaining, it must be recalled that one of the great difficulties in clearly defining scope in education has been the failure to distinguish between working conditions and educational policy. Virtually all contracts and statutes, including those containing restrictions reducing the scope of bargaining as regards educational policy matters, do contain clauses that mandate bargaining over working conditions. A clear line between educational policy and teacher working conditions has never been drawn. In the first phase of bargaining, the issue of class size symbolized the problem. Boards of education held that class size was a matter of educational policy and therefore not subject to bargaining, while the unions insisted that class size was a working condition, subject to negotiations. Now that so many contracts contain class-size provisions, the debate over this specific subject is moot, but the general question remains.* On an overall level, Arvid

---

*Charles R. Perry and Wesley A. Wildman, for instance, also emphasize that while in private employment, issues dealing with

Anderson suggests it would be a mistake to attempt to distinguish specifically between working conditions and educational policy.

> While statutory definitions and agency procedures for resolving scope questions are helpful, there are limits both in terms of practicality and wisdom as to completely spelling out and defining all of the parameters of collective bargaining in the public sector. Mature and responsible bargainers will see the value of joint deliberation and consultation with professional employees on all sorts of subjects regardless of whether or not they are "mandatory" subjects of collective bargaining. Obviously, school professionals have an important input to make in the determination of school curriculum, as well as how to deal with disruptive children, problems of narcotics in the schools and all sorts of other social problems, but again some matters of educational policy are too broad an area of public concern to be defined and determined solely by the methods of collective bargaining. For example, I do not believe that the question of school desegregation, which has been an overriding concern to the courts of the United States, to the President, Governors and Mayors and to the various state legislatures and to school boards throughout the country, should be resolved solely by collective bargaining. Too many interests are involved.[52]

In 1968 Michael H. Moskow pointed out the core of the problem, and his observation still holds meaning today.

> Another difficulty with an all-inclusive approach to the scope of negotiations is that no distinction is made between purely professional matters such as curriculum research, textbooks, teaching machines and audio-visual aids and bread and butter items such as teacher salaries and working conditions.[53]

---

transfer rights of the employee come under the heading of working conditions. However, in school systems, particularly in urban schools, transfers deal with educational policy, which is sometimes related to staff integration patterns, and with teacher experience. For general discussion, see their chapter on policies and working conditions, in The Impact of Negotiations in Public Education: The Evidence from the Schools (Worthington, Ohio: Charles A. Jones Publishing Co., 1970), pp. 178-85.

Indeed, Lieberman and Moskow once made the perceptive point that "educational policy is rarely defined; in some cases the definition seems to be that it consists of whatever the school administration does not want to negotiate."[54] They concluded that "it is extremely difficult to determine where working conditions leave off and education policy begins. Theoretically and practically the two are closely interrelated in many ways."[55]

Trying to define the difference between working conditions and educational policy seems to become even more confusing when those who evidently prefer a limited policy-making role for teachers concede at the same time that certain policy areas should be subject to negotiations. According to William J. Kilberg, writing in the Maryland Law Review in 1970, the scope must be restricted in those areas where unilateral decision-making is essential or where bilateral decision-making is not appropriate. He argued that "strategic level decisions" dealing with what is to be taught, who is to be educated and where schools are to be located are inappropriate subjects for the bargaining process.[56] He would, for example, have excluded from negotiations such subjects as curriculum and textbook selection. Nevertheless, Kilberg went on to argue for flexibility, even suggesting that teaching methodology should not be a matter left to the unilateral control of the school board. Adding further to the dilemma of just what the scope ought to be, Kilberg stated the following:

> Subjects such as teacher facilities and free periods for class preparations because of their impact on teacher working conditions should remain open for collective negotiations. There are certain subjects of a hybrid nature, such as class size, which may be viewed as matters of educational policy but whose impact on working conditions for teachers is so great that they ought to remain bargainable.[57]

Even though Kilberg called for so-called "strategic level decisions" to be removed from the bargaining process, he tended to undermine the thrust of his argument by asserting that certain subjects are of a "hybrid nature." Kilberg's view has been highlighted here, to underscore the fact that even those who want to prohibit teacher access to decision making in educational policy matters have a difficult time in clearly defining the distinction between working conditions and educational policy. In any case, by employing Kilberg's reasoning, it is easy to see how a number of educational policy issues would be, at the least, ruled as permissive subjects for negotiations by state labor boards.

The issue will also remain cloudy if states attempt to follow a balance-of-interests approach; that is, the distinction between educational policy and working conditions will become simply matters for academic debate (which may already be the case). A balance of interest has been defined as "a satisfactory balance . . . [being] struck by weighing the impact of permitting bargaining on the school board/community relationship against the impact of not permitting bargaining on the harmony of the school board/teacher relationship."[58]

Thus we have seen that with the evolution of bargaining, unions have come to play an increased role in the determination of policy, and that in the case of several typical contract provisions, their interests have proved to be in direct conflict with those of poor and minority groups. Of course, the extent to which school boards and their role in the negotiating process are themselves representative of poor and minority interests is a vital aspect of this issue. Chapters 4 and 5 examine this question.

NOTES

1. Mario Fantini, "Community Participation," in The Politics of Urban Education, edited by Marilyn Gittell and Alan G. Hevesi (New York: Praeger Publishers, 1969), p. 45.

2. David S. Seeley, "The 1972 Teacher Contract Negotiations" (mimeographed, New York: Public Education Association, 1972) p. 7.

3. "New Teacher Contract Under Negotiation," District of Columbia Citizens for Better Public Education Bulletin Board, March 1974, pp. 1-5.

4. Interview with Dr. Cornelius Golightly, President of the Detroit Board of Education, in Detroit, Mich., on June 20, 1974.

5. Agreement Between the Board of Education of the District of Columbia and the Washington Teachers Union, effective June 1971 through March 1974, pp. 39-40.

6. Ibid., p. 42.

7. Ibid., p. 22.

8. Ibid., pp. 22-23.

9. Ibid., pp. 50-51.

10. Ibid., p. 14.

11. Agreement Between the Board of Education of the City of Newark and the Newark Teachers Union, Local 481, American Federation of Teachers, AFL-CIO, Newark, N.J., effective February 1, 1973 through January 31, 1976, p. 59.

12. Ibid., p. 42.

13. Ibid., p. 12.

14. Ibid., p. 2.

15. Ibid., p. 59.

16. Ibid., p. 57.

17. Ibid., p. 57.

18. Ibid., pp. 28-29.

19. Agreement between the Board of Education of the School District of the City of Detroit and the Detroit Federation of Teachers, Local 231, American Federation of Teachers, AFL-CIO, Detroit, Mich., effective July 1, 1973 through July 1, 1974, pp. 5-6.

20. Ibid., pp. 6-7.

21. Ibid., pp. 49-50.

22. Ibid., p. 17.

23. Ibid., p. 18.

24. Ibid., pp. 18-19.

25. Ibid., pp. 9-10.

26. Ibid., p. 20.

27. Ibid., p. 21.

28. Joseph M. Cronin, The Control of Urban Schools: Perspective on the Power of Educational Reformers (New York: The Free Press, 1973), p. 198.

29. Alan Rosenthal, Pedagogues and Power: Teacher Groups in School Politics (Syracuse: Syracuse University Press, 1969). See Chapter 7, pp. 154-73.

30. Agreement between the Board of Education of the City School District of New York and the United Federation of Teachers, Local 2, American Federation of Teachers, AFL-CIO Covering Day School Classroom Teachers, etc., New York, N.Y., effective September 9, 1972 through September 9, 1975, p. 92.

31. Ibid., p. 92.

32. Ibid., p. 23.

33. Ibid., p. 79.

34. Ibid., p. 90.

35. Ibid., pp. 92-93.

36. "Teacher Collective Bargaining: Who Runs the Schools?" Fordham Urban Law Journal 2 (1973-74): 505-560.

37. Robert Gorman, remarks made in seminar entitled "Collective Bargaining," Harvard University, January 1974.

38. Edward B. Shils and C. Taylor Whittier, Teachers, Administrators, and Collective Bargaining (New York: Thomas Y. Crowell, 1968), p. 362.

39. Gorman, op. cit.

40. Robert D. Helsby, "A Political System for a Political World in Public Sector Labor Relations," Labor Law Journal 24 (August 1973): 504-511.

41. Donald H. Wollett, "The Coming Revolution in Public School Management," Michigan Law Review 67 (March 1969): 1031-32.

42. Harry H. Wellington and Ralph K. Winter, Jr., "Structuring Collective Bargaining in Public Employment," Yale Law Journal 79 (April 1970): 856.

43. Harry T. Edwards, "The Emerging Duty to Bargain in the Public Sector," Michigan Law Review 71 (April 1973): 916.

44. Lee C. Shaw and Theodore R. Clark, Jr., "The Practical Differences between Public and Private Sector Collective Bargaining," UCLA Law Review 19 (1971-72): 881.

45. Derek C. Bok and John T. Dunlop, Labor and the American Community (New York: Simon and Schuster, 1970), p. 323.

46. Donald H. Wollett, "The Bargaining Process in the Public Sector: What Is Bargainable?" Oregon Law Review 51 (Fall 1971): 177-90.

47. See Ralph P. Dupont and Robert D. Tobin, "Teachers Negotiations into the Seventies," William and Mary Law Review 12 (Summer 1971): 711-49.

48. Bok and Dunlop, op. cit., p. 226.

49. Ibid.

50. Ida Klaus, "The Evolution of a Collective Bargaining Relationship in Public Education: New York City's Changing Seven-Year History," Michigan Law Review 67 (March 1969): 1066.

51. Hy Kornbluh, "Bargaining The Goals of Education and Teachers," Changing Education (Fall 1973) p. E-2.

52. Arvid Anderson, "School Policy and Collective Bargaining" (mimeographed, Madison: University of Wisconsin, 1973), pp. 18-19.

53. Michael H. Moskow, Teachers and Unions (Philadelphia: University of Pennsylvania Press, 1968), p. 224.

54. Myron Lieberman and Michael H. Moskow, Collective Negotiations for Teachers (Chicago: Rand McNally and Co., 1966), p. 227.

55. Ibid., p. 220.

56. William J. Kilberg, "Appropriate Subjects for Bargaining in Local Government Relations," Maryland Law Review 30 (Summer 1970): 195.

57. Ibid., p. 197.

58. Grant F. Shipley, "Determining the Scope of Bargaining under the Indiana Education Employment Relations Act," Indiana Law Journal 49 (Spring 1974): 460-81.

THE POLICY ROLES
OF SCHOOL BOARDS
AND THREE NEW CLASSES
OF EXPERTS

. . . education in New York City has become amazingly insulated from public controls. The claim that only the professionals can make competent judgements has been accepted. *

Undoubtedly, one of the major questions to be pursued in considering whether the bargaining structure excludes citizens from the decision-making process centers on the board of education. Interviews conducted for this study with a number of individuals disclosed that many people were concerned about the lack of citizen access to the bargaining process; yet one contention was consistently put forth by many of these people: elected boards represent the community. In this view, if the board fails to respond to community wishes, the electorate is supposed to be able to unseat board members at the next election, or in the case of appointed boards to unseat the mayor. Thus, in some respects, criticizing the bargaining structure goes to the heart of representative democracy in public education.

This chapter addresses the question of the extent to which school boards represent community interests on three levels: (1) the obvious electoral and procedural under-representation of poor and minority groups is noted; (2) the lack of substantive participation by boards in the formulation of educational policy is explored; and (3) the emergence

---

*Marilyn Gittell, "Professionalism and Public Participation in Educational Policy-Making: New York City," in The Politics of Urban Education, edited by Marilyn Gittell and Alan G. Hevesi (New York: Praeger Publishers, 1969), p. 156.

of still another class of professionals who remove the bargaining process still further from the control of both the boards and the community
is indicated.

In its broadest terms the question of the representativeness of
school boards can be asked in Harold Laswell's classic question: "Who
gets what, when, how?"[1] There can be no question but that, tradition-
ally and presently, the system of majority-rule elections typical in
American communities inadequately represents poor and minority
groups. Their numerical under-representation on boards of education
is readily apparent in both urban and rural school districts. Two of
the most recent documentations of this situation are the following. A
1974 report of the U.S. Commission on Civil Rights, entitled Toward
Quality Education for Mexican-Americans, statistically documents the
unrepresentative character of the boards of education serving large
numbers of Chicano students. The boards tend to be overwhelmingly
Anglo even where there are large numbers of Chicano residents. New
Mexico was the only state in the Southwest with Chicano school board
membership proportionate to Chicano enrollment.[2] In a similar way
the Fifth Circuit Court, in Zimmer vs. McKeithan (1973), found that
at-large elections for the school board and the police jury in East Car-
roll Parish, Louisiana, work to keep blacks off such boards and are
therefore unconstitutional. Additional suits similar to this are pending
in other states. *

Furthermore, and not surprisingly, there is much evidence that
those who are elected to these unrepresentative school boards fail to
provide these "disenfranchised" groups with adequate hearings and representation. The entire civil rights struggle, centering on the reform
of educational programs offered to poor and minority students, demonstrates this inadequacy. Similarly, the drive for community control
of public schools, the development of minority-controlled alternative
schools, and the protests of parents against certain contractual provisions, as documented in Chapter 3 of this book, confirm this point.
Numerous scholars have documented the ways in which poor and minority groups are shortchanged by the political process that currently decides who gets what, when and how. † Admittedly, a variety of

---

*In March 1975 the Center for Law and Education, Harvard Uni-
versity, filed a class action suit on behalf of the black voters of Boston,
charging that the use of at-large elections for the School Committee
discriminates against black citizens. Black Voters, Rose Jolley et al.
vs. John McDonough, the Boston School Committee, et al.

†Robert Lyke goes so far as to say that "no centralized urban
board of education is likely to be very responsive" to community organizations that are placing demands before it. In his essay,

proposals has been made for reforming both the electoral process and the "due process" between elections, in order to see that these groups are more equitably represented in the future; nonetheless, it is clear that such changes are extremely difficult to achieve, and perhaps even impossible, given the nature of the political constituencies in many urban and rural districts. Until such reforms can be instituted and proven to work, other mechanisms for minority representation in the determination of educational policy must be considered, as in this study. Otherwise, the main mechanism by which poor and minority groups can effect these determinations will continue to be that of sporadic protest and violent unrest. Michael B. Katz has called attention to this failure of boards of education to deal with the interests of poor and minority groups, as follows:

> The hostile reaction of school boards like Boston's in the
> 1960s to the problem of de facto segregation . . . reveal-
> ed how long-standing insensitivity of a school system to
> its poor clientele had hardened into a pattern of interact-
> ing with community groups. Incident after incident sug-
> gested that school boards simply did not care to try to
> understand the aspiration of some black people; it appears
> simply, that the wishes of black people did not matter
> much. That open confrontation has now broken out in some

"Representation and Urban School Boards," Lyke places emphasis on two factors that account for the either ineffective or nonexistent representation of a high number of urban blacks and of the poor. First, he says that political parties have hardly any role in school politics; this results in a missing pressure group, which should be forcing the school bureaucracy to respond to new community groups representing alienated citizens. Other city agencies, he argues, are at least exposed to such political pressure. Second, he concludes that even when board members respond to demands, they find it much easier to relate to the pressures of traditional interest groups, such as teacher groups, business organizations, and PTAs, since set procedures are followed and negotiations are in the main private, thereby giving board members a sense of control over bargaining and its outcome. See Robert Lyke, "Representation and Urban School Boards," in Community Control of Schools, edited by Henry M. Levin (New York: Clarion 1970.) Also see Joseph M. Cronin and Richard M. Hailer, Organizing a School System for Diversity: A Study of the Boston School Department (Boston: McBer, 1970); Marilyn Gittell and T. Edward Hollander, Six Urban School Districts (New York: Praeger Publishers, 1968); Leonard J. Fein, "Community Schools and Social Theory: The Limits of Universalism," in Community Control of Schools, op. cit.

areas should surprise no one. It is the legacy of school
government cut off from and insensitive to the community
it serves. [3]

The following sections of this chapter will concentrate on the
much less apparent fact that, even if school boards could be made more
representative of poor and minority groups, the boards themselves
would have limited direct power to change educational policy. If the
boards turn out to have minor or decreasing power in the definition of
policy, then elected reforms to change the makeup of the boards will
still be inadequate to the task of giving the community more say in educational matters.

BOARDS OF EDUCATION AND THE OLD PROFESSIONALS:
WHO WAS IN CONTROL?

A few years ago the Gallup Poll, after interviewing school board
members around the country, came up with this finding:

In most communities, school board members say they are
overwhelmed by problems of immediate concern—finding
enough money in the budget to meet school needs, trying
to keep up with population growth, with new buildings and
classrooms, meeting the problems of teacher shortages,
seeking able and experienced teachers within budget limitations. These tasks occupy most of the time of the nation's school boards. . . In many communities the local
school board does not devote much time to the discussion
of the curriculum or to innovative practices, since these
are left largely up to the judgement of the superintendent,
principals, and other members of the administrative
staff. [4]

The significant point in this finding was the dominant role played
in policy making by the school administration. Several studies of educational policy-making support this same conclusion. Koerner, in
Who Controls American Education, found that

the balance of power in most local systems is strongly in
favor of the superintendent of schools and of the administration generally, in large part because of the failures of
the school board and local teachers, both of whom in my
view, should exercise a greater voice in policy than they
do. [5]

In an earlier study, Roscoe C. Martin concluded that the superintendent was an omnipotent power in the setting of policy:

> He is at least as much a policy maker as he is a manager
> in the narrow sense; for he enjoys an expertise, a pro-
> fessional reputation and a community position which com-
> bine to give him an almost irresistible voice in school
> affairs. [6]

Martin noted that the rise of the superintendent to power resulted in the simultaneous decline of the position of the school board. [7] More importantly, historians have documented that the rise of professionals was intended to diminish the power of the more political school boards, which were subject to community pressures. *

In a study covering Baltimore, Chicago, Detroit, New York, Philadelphia and St. Louis, Gittell and Hollander discovered that rarely did the school board ever control the making of school policy. Instead, policy making was largely under the dominance of small groups of administrators within the school bureaucracy. [8] Gittell has written extensively on the New York City school system and she has underscored the declining participation of the board in shaping policies:

---

*For an excellent discussion of the historical development and emergence of the professional educator as a pervasive power in public schooling see Michael B. Katz, Class, Bureaucracy and Schools: The Illusion of Educational Change in America (New York: Praeger Publishers, 1971). Also see Katz's The Irony of Early School Reform (Boston: Beacon Press, 1968). Joseph M. Cronin's work, The Control of Urban Schools: Perspective on the Power of Educational Reformers (New York: The Free Press, 1973), also provides a succinct account of the same development treated by Katz. Cronin has provided a concise summary of what happened with the superintendency at the beginning of the century, as follows:

> Most of the older cities by 1900 had abolished ward or
> community school boards and transferred their powers to
> central boards. When that was not enough, reformers
> tried to reduce the size of the board and transferred many
> of the more sensitive duties—teacher nomination, textbook
> selection, in addition to teacher supervision—to a super-
> intendent. During the twentieth century the superintendents
> have asserted and won chief executive status by assuming
> additional responsibilities for school business management.
> But the trend to delegate more power to professional staff
> members can be discerned in the last quarter of the nine-
> teenth century. p. 9.

As the school system has grown larger and more complex and as policies demand more specialized knowledge, the board has had to withdraw from an effective
policy role. The bureaucracy and special interest
groups have gained power by means of their expertise,
while the board, lacking expertise, has lost power.[9]

Furthermore, numerous scholars have indicated that the lack of
expertise on the part of school boards is not entirely accidental. Greenbaum and Cronin, in studying school-board decision making in Boston
from October 1967 to July 1969, found that the school committee was
responsible for initiating only three policy issues, and further observed that

the administration jealously guards its often unused education prerogatives by resisting the development of any
serious school committee structure which might permit
the development of educational expertise on the part of
the committee members.[10]

Joseph Pois comments as follows on the flow of information to school-
board members:

The general superintendent's ability to channel the Board's
deliberations has been enhanced immeasurably by the
practice of having the agenda for board meetings consist
almost exclusively of reports transmitted by the general
superintendent for board consideration. In effect, this
places the general superintendent in the position of initiating most matters and may make the individual member
feel that he has a secondary or subordinate part in determining the scope, priorities, or emphasis of the sessions
in which he participates. The large number of pro forma
items that necessarily encumber board meetings as a
result of the allocation of responsibilities makes the
general superintendent's control of the agenda far more
defensible than it might at first appear. . . .
Manifestly, a board should avail itself of the factual
material and viewpoints emanating from the general
superintendent and his subordinates. Yet if this is the
exclusive source of systematic inquiry and analysis concerning the school system, the board's decision-making
must inevitably be determined in large measure by the
attitudes and concepts of the bureaucracy. Such a result
is not reconcilable with the premise, frequently expressed,
that the board brings an independent point of view to bear

upon school issues and problems. Although administrators
should not and cannot be insulated from the policy-making
process, this does not mean that a governing body should
have no regular sources of information and study other
than the administrative personnel whose judgements, values, and even competence it supposedly subjects to scru-
tiny. The contrary may be argued far more persuasively
in the private sector where the concerns of a board are
ordinarily more limited and where public policy is not the
transcendent consideration.

The lack of adequate information is bound to confirm a
board member's tendency to take refuge in the more hum-
drum matters while dealing gingerly with difficult or elu-
sive problems, or amiably concurring in the desires of
the superintendent. The layman who "takes on" the professional frequently assumes a calculated risk of being
rebuffed decisively—if not put to rout—by the expert who
has ready access to the pertinent data or background
material.

The Chicago Board, when it does seek to tap the informa-
tional, statistical, and research resources of the school
system, is ordinarily expected to use its general superintendent as the point of contact. Although this may be
justified on the basis of protocol or recognition of lines
of responsibility in the administrative hierarchy, the end
result is that the flow of information is subject to screen-
ing, selection, or restatement by the general superintendent. As organizations expand in size, it becomes less
tenable to contend that the chief administrative or executive officer should be the sole conduit for the transmittal
of data or analyses to the governing body. [11]

A 1974 study by Badi Foster, "Democracy and Change: The Performance of School Board Members," bears out the earlier perceptions
of Pois. Foster looked at two school boards, Chicago and Minneapolis.
With respect to Chicago, he concluded as follows:

Board members have been ineffective in Chicago because
they lack the skills necessary to formulate and enact
changes or they don't want to make them. For example,
Board members don't know how to reorganize their ar-
chaic financial system and they have ignored opportunities
for assistance. They do, however, have the power to
redistrict the school system to deal with segregated
schools created by residential patterns, but apprarently

they don't want to act.

Power as incapacity is illustrated in the attempt by Superintendent Redmond and the School Board to impose decentralization on the staff. Its questionable progress is probably due to the lack of significant involvement by staff members in planning for decentralization and the patterns of inertia and dependence among staff members which carried over from the previous administration. [12]

While finding Minneapolis a somewhat more open system, nonetheless, Foster states that the Board members lack the required skills to bring about changes.* Foster concludes that

school boards in Chicago and Minneapolis suffer from the lack of appropriate measures and the incapacity that results when power is exercised without the means, the consciousness, the creativity or the ability to link with others in trying to set policy for problems in the schools. [13]

Interestingly enough, in recent times school boards have played a large role in one critical area: school desegregation; witness the stance taken in 1975 by the Boston School Committee. Indeed, desegregation was one of the only areas in which Greenbaum and Cronin found that the Boston School Committee took an active role. [14] Robert L. Crain and David Street found, in their study of eight school systems

----

*Foster's paper contains two lengthy interviews with one board member from each city. The interviews furnish an important insight into how board members perceive their position. This study further provides a very interesting contrast between the central administrations of the two cities. It is noteworthy that among his recommendations, Foster calls upon school board members to become involved in the bargaining process:

a) Board members should enroll in one of the courses in negotiations and collective bargaining offered by the local or regional business schools, departments of labor relations, corporations, unions, or

b) School boards should conduct simulated bargaining sessions, with board members alternating roles.

c) School board members should establish formal procedures for discovering the concerns and priorities of those with whom they will eventually bargain. Systemwide meetings for the purpose of discussing competing views and issues prior to actual bargaining would provide board members with a better sense of whom they are dealing with and what would be acceptable to them in view of their demands.

faced with desegregation, that boards become involved in decisions
affecting integration. On the other hand, they underlined that outside
the area of race, the superintendent's rule was supreme.

> On many issues—for example, curriculum construction,
> textbook selection, or design of facilities—the superin-
> tendent's judgements generally go unchallenged, not
> only because they usually fall into areas of indifference
> but also because the superintendent's accumulation of
> detailed information, his technical background, and his
> appeals to standard or good practice argue well for hon-
> oring his professional claims. On such issues, the
> superintendent in effect runs the schools. Any criticism
> in these areas may cause the superintendent to accuse
> the board of interference with his administrative role.[15]

Equally significant, their findings disclosed the administrator's
resistance to change in general and integration in particular, as
follows:

> Of course, these reactions are common to all organiza-
> tions which must meet criticism, but the educators go
> further than most public officials in reacting defensively
> to political demands. Educational administrators are in-
> sistent on defining themselves as professionals and have
> an entrenched ideology that grants lay control but stresses
> the importance of the teaching certificate and "education-
> al experience" as the boundary between the expert and
> the layman. In part, the response to the demands for
> integration is only another instance of the professional's
> tendency—developed through generations of conflict over
> political interference, progressive education, charges
> of Communism in the schools, and other issues—to per-
> ceive any criticism as an "attack upon education."[16]

Crain and Street further identify other factors that serve to restrict the school's ability to meet the needs of community groups as
follows:

> These systems are overcentralized in the sense that
> standardized curricula and administration by formula do
> not provide enough fiscal and administrative autonomy to
> permit "decentralized" administrators to vary their pro-
> grams to local needs with any real facility. Yet they are
> undercentralized in the sense that it is very difficult for

decisions made at the top of the organization to alter the
traditional operating procedures. This is particularly
the case in cities where principals or other personnel
have become highly entrenched in their positions; the
man who has been principal of the same school for twenty
years is not responsive to supervision. Commitment to
the status quo is often heightened by inbreeding and by
the associations of principals and other personnel which
act as mutual protective associations. [17]

Thus it would appear that even when the board initiates policy the professional bureaucracy can stand in the way of implementation.

In many instances board members began to question the infallibility of the superintendent. The nature of this clash between board
members and superintendent is sharply revealed in the perceptions of
a former board member of the Washington, D.C., school system.
Martha Swaim, after serving five years on the board of education, from
January 1969 to July 1974, holds a view on the "professionalism" that
is similar to the conclusions reached in the studies previously cited.

Unfortunately, most Superintendents are surprised or
annoyed when parents turn to the Board. Superintendents
get irritated with Board attempts to find out what is really
happening to policy. A Superintendent may be upset because the Board finds a policy is not being carried out.
For example, the Board may find that some kindergartens
do not have teachers. Or the Board may discover that the
policy was based on incomplete information in the first
place. For example, kindergartens may have no equipment because the inventory that management said was
there, was not.
Superintendents may also get upset on general principles.
Boards do make mistakes and propose solutions that are
impractical or too expensive. But more than that, Superintendents believe that professionals know better. "Professionals" as defined by the administration, are the people in the system, not those on the board. Superintendents,
like the education profession as a whole, have a hard time
understanding that parents and taxpayers, with the Board
as their representative, have a right to know, inspect,
and see everything that might affect their child and the
spending of their tax money. [18]

On the issue of school policy, Swaim stated as follows:

Finally, I have two rules of thumb for guidance in discussions in policy and administration. "Policy" is not
only rules and regulations and procedures for this and
that; "policy" deals with what is important to people
about schools. Second, anyone who complains about the
Board "meddling in administration" usually has some-
thing to hide. Even if the Board is proposing an imper-
fect solution to a problem, some well paid administrator
is the person who produced the problem in the first
place. [19]

The Washington situation is illustrative of the fact that at one level of
the educational power structure there is a growing tension between the
professionals at the upper echelon of the school hierarchy and the
school boards. *

In his study of two medium-sized school districts on the East
Coast, Robert Lyke, after interviewing board members, found that
most policy decisions were left to the administration:

In policy-areas that administrators are considered to
have technical competence which laymen chary to judge,
it would be difficult, if not foolhardy, to support the
citizens consistently and ignore the professional staff.
Nonetheless, the tendency of board members to abdicate
effective authority on educational policy to administrators
and teachers is a significant restriction on substantive
representation. [20]

Thus we have seen that in some cases the school boards abdicate
responsibility for policy making, while in other cases administrators
prevent them from "interfering" in policy. In practical terms the unilateral determination of policy before the rise of collective bargaining
was largely in the hands of administrators and their "expertise," and

---

*The dispute in Washington between the board and the superin-
tendent has continued. In December 1974, for instance, Barbara Sizemore, the new superintendent, suggested that a mediator be brought
in to clarify the differences between policy and administration to the
board. On the other hand, one board member was quoted as saying,
"I think the superintendent has forgotten who's responsible for the
school system," while another more pointedly declared, "It's very
clear the lady thinks she is in charge, it's going to be her way, and
there is no respect for the board from the superintendent or her staff."
Washington Post, December 13, 1974, p. C3.

not in the hands of "lay boards". While the authority of superintendents has sharply eroded because of the failure of the schools to provide effective educational programs, this decrease in their power has not been accomplished by an increase in the power of boards over policy. In the next section, the rise of a new class of professionals, who are assuming increasing influence in the determination of policy, is considered.

CLASS ONE: BOARD NEGOTIATORS

With the advent of bargaining it was not long before school boards took steps to remove themselves from participating directly in the bargaining process. Myron Lieberman, for example, has reported that in 1971-72 only 15 percent of the negotiating teams he studied were comprised of board members.[21] Essentially one of two actions were generally taken by a board: (1) it would hire a so-called labor law expert as its chief negotiator (a lawyer), or (2) it would create a new position, such as Deputy Superintendent and/or Director, in the personnel department, solely to conduct negotiations and implement contracts with all organized and recognized school employees.*

Frederick R. Livingston, a lawyer, mediator and arbitrator, has said that neither superintendents nor boards are capable of negotiating with teachers unions. With respect to superintendents, he puts it this way:

> While they may be expert at setting educational policy and
> operating the school system, superintendents generally
> have no experience, background or knowledge which en-
> ables them to cope with the difficult problem of negotiat-
> ing with teacher unions.[22]

---

*In Washington, D.C., the board in the first two contract negotiations hired an experienced private-sector management attorney. By the time of the thrid round of negotiations, the board had hired a permanent director of employer/employee relations. The director became the chief negotiator for the school board. Neither the director nor the attorney had any previous working knowledge of public school systems. This lack of familiarity with public schooling is not uncommon. The former chief negotiator for the Detroit Board of Education, and now number two in the chain of command in that school system's hierarchy, had previously worked with the National Labor Relations Board.

Regarding school boards, Livingston explains why he believes they
must turn to the labor expert, as follows:

> School board members are traditionally unpaid and have
> full-time jobs by which they earn their living. Thus un-
> like other governmental executive officers, they are not
> continuously involved in operations, and are not familiar
> with the day-to-day functioning of the school system. It
> is often difficult for them to assemble on short notice
> or on a continuous basis for crisis decisions during a
> period of intense negotiations. This sometimes results
> either in delegating policy making to the staff or in put-
> ting off decisions and thus exacerbating relations with
> teachers and making settlement more difficult to reach.
> . . .
> Finally, schools happen to be the area of governmental
> activity in which employee organization has been most
> rapid and effective in the past decade. There have emer-
> ged two strong national teacher organizations which com-
> pete vigorously with each other. . . . Each one is in-
> fluenced in its negotiating by the need to demonstrate
> that it can produce more for teachers than the other.
> This has resulted in many places in a wide disparity in
> the bargaining effectiveness between a school board and
> the union which it faces across the table. The local union
> is likely to be supported by a state and national organiza-
> tion which provides advice, staff assistance, and even
> substantial funding in the event of a crisis. It is probably
> coordinating with other teacher unions in its area, or even
> statewide, to present a common front and play off one
> school district against another.
> In most places school boards are far behind. They rely
> exclusively on their own resources, and often devote woe-
> fully little of those resources to negotiation, which, after
> all, determine the bulk of their budget. While they are
> very effective in joint lobbying efforts before the state
> legislatures, they have developed only the most minimal
> communication, much less cooperation, in bargaining.
> Incredibly, many school boards still try to negotiate
> themselves or through their regular staff, without re-
> taining competent and experienced professional labor re-
> lations advisors. [23]

In 1974 attorney James L. Rogers, speaking before the Iowa Association of School Boards about the new Iowa public employment law to

go into effect July 1, 1975, urged the boards to hire professional negotiators from the outside. [24] Attorney John H. Leddy, writing of his
negotiating experiences in the Ohio State Law Journal, is very blunt
about how he perceives the boards' participation in negotiations: "They
simply are not qualified to be bargainers." Board members, according
to Leddy, should be excluded from bargaining because "they are too
emotionally involved in their school systems to make the objective and
dispassionate decisions which are the stock in trade of a professional
negotiator."[25] Another dilemma facing the board's professional negotiator, Leddy says, occurs when the interests of the administration and
the school board do not coincide. This observation should be borne in
mind, for it tends to support previous findings that have highlighted
the administration's control of educational policy making. If Leddy
is correct, then one may assume that bargaining can sharpen the cleavage between the central administration and the board. Such a development would further undermine the role of the board in the decision
making that takes place during negotiations.

These latter remarks indicate the stress being given to the law-
yer-negotiator—he or she moves into a strategic position of authority
in the school hierarchy.* These lawyers are mainly hired only during
the period of actual negotiations. Class One also includes another type
of professional negotiator, the person holding a full-time administrative position for the school system. Daily participation in the total
bargaining process provides these school administrators with a power
position second only to that of the superintendent. In some circumstances the chief negotiator's influence may actually equal that of the
top administrative officer. Leslie Jones, for instance, formerly the
assistant suerpintendent in charge of employer-employee relations for
the Washington, D.C., school district, has said that as the chief negotiator for the board he held a strategic power base within the decision-
making structure. [26]

---

*The prominence of lawyers is not by any means limited to the
field of public education. One could argue, for instance, that a similar development has occurred in the area of school desegregation.
Black parents seeking equity in the schools have often turned to civil
rights attorneys, most notably the National Association for the Advancement of Colored People (NAACP), to obtain equal educational opportunity. It is not uncommon for the attorney to emerge as the central
decision maker in such cases, sometimes representing more of a legal
principle than the actual desires of black parents. For discussion of
this theme see Ronald R. Edmonds, "Advocating Inequity: A Critique
of the Civil Rights Attorney in Class Action Desegregation Suits," The
Black Law Journal 3 (1974): 176-83.

Disclosing a similar role of the chief negotiator for the board
in Detroit, the current president of the Board of Education, Dr. Cornelius Golightly, has suggested that during the 1973 Detroit teachers'
strike, the administrative officer in charge of negotiations was really
in command of the board's position.[27] That is, the chief negotiator was
responsible for making the key decisions regarding a strike settlement.
In theory, the professional board negotiators can handle only bargaining, while school boards strictly control the actions of these negotiators; but in reality the nature of the bargaining process, the complexity
of the language of bargaining, and the lay status of board members, and
their part-time commitment to the task, all tend to lead to an actual
transfer of power.

In summary, this rising influence of a lawyer negotiator and/or
school administrative officer on the handling of negotiations has had
the effect of creating a new class of professionals in the school administrative hierarchy. This group of new experts wields enormous influence in the operations of large urban school systems. Simply put, this
development removes the board further away from the crucial arena
in which far-reaching decisions are made. Instead, the professionals
decide major questions in both the formal and informal process of collective bargaining. There is a new group of "technocrats" emerging
within public education. *

While not specifically speaking to the rise of the new professional

---

*Although this study deals primarily with teacher negotiations,
it is noteworthy that it is not only teachers who are represented by
recognized bargaining agents: custodians, cafeteria workers, secre-
taries, and in some cases principals are represented by unions. The
chief negotiator for the board is generally responsible for negotiations
with all these employees, which gives even more importance to the
pivotal role of this new class.

In much more national and global terms, John Kenneth Galbraith,
in his work Economics and the Public Purpose (Boston: Houghton Mifflin, 1973), deals with the rise of the technostructure. On its ability
to be decisive in establishing major policy, Galbraith states, "Papal
infallibility was powerfully served by the fact that the Holy Father defined error. The assurance that public policy will infallibly serve the
technostructure and the planning system is similarly attested by the
ability of the technostructure to define the public interest." pp. 162–63.
I do not think it is an exaggeration to suggest that the new technostructure in public education—third-party neutrals, teachers unions, and
board negotiators—sometimes claim they are representing the public
interest in the manner indicated by Galbraith.

technocrats in teacher negotiations, Clyde Summers in the <u>Yale Law Journal</u> (1974) has described the exclusive character of the bargaining structure in the public sector. His remarks point up the representative- ness problem as follows:

> Other groups interested in the size of or allocation of
> the budget are not present during negotiations and often
> are not even aware of the proposals being discussed.
> Their concerns are not articulated and their counter-
> vailing political pressures are not felt except by proxy
> through the city representative at the bargaining table. [28]

These remarks take on added meaning once it has been noted, as earli- er in this chapter, that the board itself is far-removed from the actual conduct of negotiations. So far this chapter has stressed 1) the unrep- resentative character of boards of education, 2) the lack of participa- tion by boards in formulating educational policy, and 3) the removal from direct participation in the bargaining process.

ADDITIONAL DEVELOPMENTS

Nonetheless, I do not wish to imply that boards of education make no decisions regarding bargaining. Boards may directly enter the pro- cess over a controversial issue. In 1975, for example, a situation arose in Washington, D.C., in which the board of education insisted in negotiations that teachers work a longer school day; this demand ema- nated from the board rather than the chief negotiator for the board or the administrative negotiating team. Still, two observations must be made. Participation in one or even a few controversial issues by any board does not provide substantive involvement in the overall delibera- tions, in which the outcome, as a result of the expansion of scope, can leave many major policy decisions in the hands of the administration and the union. Second, such involvement in no way resolves the issue of the exclusive two-party bargaining structure.

Two other factors in the general decline of board power deserve brief attention. The first may have a far-reaching impact on bargain- ing and the control, such as it is, of the local school board. Joseph M. Cronin has argued that in the future, money for education will in- creasingly be found at the state level. He predicts that teacher organi- zations, given this financial development, will turn toward statewide negotiated agreements. [29] Should such a move occur, it is my judge- ment that the influence of union staff and board negotiators would

become greater than it already is under the present structure. * There
is as yet no statewide bargaining, although in February 1975 there was
a statewide teachers strike in Delaware that was directed toward the
state legislature. In Michigan, the Michigan Federation of Teachers
has given support to regional coordinated bargaining, while in New
York a committee of the New York State legislature this past year recommended consideration of a regional coalition of teachers to bargain
with a regional coalition of school boards. 30

A second point, which is not immediately related to collective
bargaining, has to do with recent actions taken by federal and local
courts in the area of school policy. Various decisions have encroached
on local board control. Clearly, the landmark case in modern times
is the 1954 Brown vs. Board of Education decision regarding school
desegregation. Of equal significance, some have argued, is the U.S.
Supreme Court decision in Lau vs. Nichols, regarding the educational
rights of non-English-speaking Chinese children in San Francisco. †
Summarizing the impact of a few of these court decisions, William R.
Hazard, in an article in Phi Delta Kappan, has concluded as follows:

> The policy making role of local school boards is modified
> by the capacity of the courts to examine educational issues
> and adopt positions which effectively pre-empt the boards'
> policies on these matters. Through federal and state leg-
> islation, court decisions and local opinions, the law clear-
> ly denies the mythology that says, "educational policy
> making is the function of the local school boards."31

In a related development that could have long-range implications
for collective bargaining in public education, a Philadelphia parents

---

*For an analysis of the possible implications of state financing
on collective bargaining, see Larry G. Simon, "The School Finance
Decisions: Collective Bargaining and Future Finance Systems," Yale
Law Journal 82 (January 1973): 409-460.

†To gain one perspective on this decision, see May Ying Chen,
"Lau vs. Nichols: Landmark in Bilingual Education," Bridge, February 1975, pp. 3-7; and for a general discussion on legal developments
surrounding bilingual education, see Erica B. Grubb's article, "Breaking the Language Barrier: The Right to Bilingual Education," Harvard
Civil Rights/Civil Liberties Law Review 9 (January 1974): 53-93. In a
related matter, a district court in Serra et al. vs. Portals has directed the Portals School District in New Mexico to "provide for the specialized educational needs of its Spanish surnamed students."

union has filed suit against the city school board and the Philadelphia Federation of Teachers to prevent them from bargaining jointly over educational policy issues. The suit is being handled by Paul Tractenberg of the Education Law Center in Newark. Tractenberg has said that the Philadelphia teachers agreement is representative of a broad trend in teacher negotiations in which there have been large-scale encroachments through bargaining into the educational decision-making process.[32] The suit itself makes a broad attack on the existing bargaining agreement in the following statement:

> In a five-front attack on the contract, the complaint disapproves: the shared responsibility over both the nature and the funding of school extracurricular activities between a school principal or the Board and a PFT committee. Fernandez pointed out that the PFT enjoys veto power over decisions it won't endorse, and consequently several of the city's junior high schools are without extracurricular programs because of quibbling between the two parties.
> . . . the contract's transfer policy, which bars the involuntary transfer of teachers with more than one year's experience. Tractenberg said this clause curtails faculty desegregation efforts.
> . . . the right of a non-tenured teacher to seek third-party arbitration if dismissed for "just cause" by the school system.
> . . . the use of School Board/PFT "joint committees" to evaluate placement and graduation certificates for the educable mentally retarded in public schools.
> . . . the requirement that "prior adequate negotiations" between the Board and the PFT precede any decision affecting "working conditions of employees."[33]

Arguing a position similar to that of Harry H. Wellington and Ralph K. Winter, Jr.,[34] Tractenberg says that the bargaining process provides a private organization the opportunity to shape public policy decisions, which are constitutionally under the board's domain.[35] As of this writing, no decision has been rendered in this suit. The subject of this case and the organizing of a parents union serve to underscore the rising dissatisfaction with the bargaining structure in urban areas.

TWO ADDITIONAL NEW CLASSES OF EXPERTS

Even after considering the limited policy role of school boards, the rise of Class One board negotiations, and the emergence of parent discontent with these developments and the rise of teachers unions, the complexity of recent changes in the distribution of power to make educational policy is sharply understated. In addition to the recent centralization of power in the hands of board negotiators, the increasing policy role of two other professional groups must be noted.

Class Two: Union Staff

As the collective bargaining process has evolved and become increasingly centralized, union professionals have expanded their roles and power. Union access to decision making falls for the most part into the hands of the union staff leadership. It is the union bureaucracy, not the rank and file, that gains the real degree of authority in this aspect of the bargaining relationship.

Indeed, a case can be made for the idea that not infrequently the joint union/board committees provide more power to union staff than to teachers. This is so because most of these committees are designed to operate on a central level, with business being conducted between the central union office and the central school administration office. To be sure, rank-and-file union members are often, if not always, appointed to serve on these policy committees; but the union staff, including paid elected officials, has a dominant voice in determining the union's position in these committee meetings. In any case, the major point to make is that this phase of the ongoing bargaining relationship can and often does provide the union leadership in large urban systems with a "hidden" and extremely important entry into decision making.

There are three main processes in which union professionals exercise dominant control. Ida Klaus has identified these areas, which are all interrelated: (1) formal negotiations process resulting in written agreements; (2) day-to-day application and implementation of the agreements at the school level of the terms agreed upon;* (3) continuous consultation between the parties, extending beyond the scope of formal bargaining and dealing with subjects of mutual concern that are either not properly within the scope of negotiations or not susceptible

---

*As a former union staff person in a major urban school system, I can report that this aspect of the bargaining relationship can lead to powerful influence with the central school administration. Many significant decisions are made over the phone between the union staff and the administration.

to being properly resolved at the bargaining table. [36] The latter point is particularly important in fully ascertaining the day-to-day influence of the union.

As union professionals gain power, the chances increase that there will be a displacement of rank-and-file goals and that Robert Michel's "iron law of oligarchy" will prove accurate. When this occurs, it may be detrimental to the interests of the larger community and teachers themselves. One important effect of the rise of Class Two is that the particular problems and interests of teachers at the school-building level often do not receive high priority. Equally important from the perspective of this study is the fact that where the central union staff and small groups of teachers disagree about cooperating with the community, the former usually win. Some exceptions have arisen, and these are noted in Chapters 5 and 6.

Class Three: Professional Neutrals

I close this chapter by introducing a new issue, an issue that began to emerge in my mind after I had made a number of interviews for this study. Although the initial concern was about the policy and bargaining roles of the unions and boards of education, it became clear that another important group with a stake in the bilateral structure was

---

Another critical area not covered here has to do with the rising political influence of teacher groups in state politics. Mario Fantini has pointed out what occurred in New York State in efforts to secure a new requirement for teacher certification. According to him, a compromise was finally worked out between the AFT and the NEA in drawing up new requirements. Without detailing an account of what happened, it is important to take note of Fantini's observation regarding the union's demand that the bargaining agent be involved in drafting the requirements: "Almost all educators would agree that no reform is possible without teacher participation. . . However, there is a difference between teacher participation and teacher control as provided by a professional union. . . . By insisting that the bargaining agent be the key participant and not teachers who may be elected by classroom teachers specifically for the program being considered, the agent of the union takes priority." For a full discussion, see Mario Fantini, What's Best for the Children? Resolving the Power Struggle between Parents and Teachers (New York: Doubleday, Anchor Press, 1974), pp. 119-25.

emerging in the public sector. This group, consisting of third-party neutrals, is called Class Three.

States having comprehensive bargaining laws for public employees usually provide for a state agency—a public labor relations board—to oversee the enforcement and implementation of the law. These state labor boards are given wide responsibility under state statutes. Among their functions are conducting elections; making unit determinations and resolving impasses; and helping to shape the scope of bargaining, an issue of paramount concern in this study. As we have seen in New York, the Public Employment Relations Board (PERB) continues to play a vital role in determining the outcome of negotiations. Under the revised public employment bill in New Jersey, the Public Relations Employment Commission (PERC) has the authority to determine the scope in appeals cases. Another, and more interesting, aspect of the new law is that PERC, in cooperation with the Institute of Management and Labor Relations at Rutgers University, will develop a grogram to train the bargaining parties to "discharge their employee-management relations responsibilities in the public interest."[37] The people who work for these agencies fall into two categories: (1) those under governor's appointments, which often extend beyond the tenure of the appointing governors, such as the position of chairperson; (2) professional staff hired by the agency. These two groups end up making decisions that can and do affect the operations of school systems. Importantly, in their role as neutrals these new professionals in public school bargaining are distantly removed from the local school district and community. One board member has put it this way:

> We'll have to assume that whoever is appointed is the
> best arbitrator available and that he'll look out for the
> interests of all people concerned about education; but the
> point is there is no place for citizen involvement in the
> whole process. . . What we have is an expanding scope
> of negotiations and we have outside influences taking over
> the process and therefore shortcircuiting any citizen
> impact.[38]

Concluding in his study that New York's PERB would have authority in deciding the scope of negotiations, Irving H. Sabghir said such influence might have far-reaching effects.[39] The Kurt L. Hanslowe and Walter E. Oberer report, which we have already referred to, also stresses the pivotal role of PERB in determining scope.[40]

In his analysis of the Indiana statute, Grant F. Shipley indicates that in reaching a balance of interest—deciding the scope—the factfinder, a third-party neutral, "may make an educational determination of which interest or balance should prevail."[41]

Up to now, reference to the neutrals has been in the context of the formal bargaining process. It must be noted that neutrals also play an instrumental part in enforcing the contract through grievance arbitration. In most instances, such grievance cases are heard through mechanisms set up by the American Arbitration Association. True, the arbitrator is supposedly limited to the subject before him or her, but the fact remains that under binding-arbitration provisions in bargaining agreements, the arbitrator is in a position of some command. Indeed the Paul Prasow study has underscored the critical part the neutral plays in public sector bargaining, in the following terms:

> More often than in the private sector, he (the interest
> neutral) must be innovative; he must plow new ground.
> He cannot function as a lifeless minor reflecting pre-
> collective negotiation practices which management may
> yearn to perpetuate but which are the target of multitudes
> of public employees in revolt. [42]

Arvid Anderson also underlines the critical role of neutrals, as follows:

> The collective bargaining table and the administrative
> procedures associated with it is a method for improving
> the conditions of employment of public employees includ-
> ing teachers and ultimately the quality of our society, but
> it will take the best efforts of and judgements of school
> administrators, teachers and neutrals to make it work in
> the public interest. [43]

In summary then, what we see emerging is the powerful influence of these new professionals, whose rise to power in the public sector is being ignored. Critics of teacher bargaining concentrate on the increasing power of the unions while failing to take note of other critical developments in the bargaining relationships. It is not without significance that of the mediators and arbitrators interviewed during the course of this study, most advocated the continuation of the present bargaining structure.

In conclusion, it is important to note the shift in the locus of power that has occurred with the emergence of the three new classes of experts described above. This development is highly significant to this study's central interest in the effect of the current bargaining structure on the ability of the community to actively participate in the definition of educational policy. The result of this shift to the locus of power is to further remove the power to determine the public interest from important segments of the public itself. The next chapter examines the origins and evolution of the community control movement, to gain further understanding of why the present bargaining structure is inadequate.

NOTES

1. Quoted by Jeffrey A Raffel, in a review of The Neighborhood-Based Politics of Education by Harry L. Summerfield, in Harvard Educational Review 42 (February 1972), p. 127.

2. U.S. Commission on Civil Rights Report: Toward Quality Education for Mexican Americans, vol. 6 (Washington, D.C.: the Commission, 1974), pp. 41-47.

3. Michael B. Katz, Class, Bureaucracy and Schools: The Illusion of Educational Change in America (New York: Praeger Publishers, 1971), pp. 116-17.

4. Quoted in James D. Koerner, Who Controls American Education? (Boston: Beacon Press, 1968), p. 125.

5. Ibid., p. 137.

6. Roscoe C. Martin, Government and the Suburban School (Syracuse: Syracuse University Press, 1962), p. 61.

7. Ibid., p. 62.

8. See T. Edward Hollander and Marilyn Gittell, Six Urban School Districts: A Comparative Study of Institutional Response, (New York: Praeger Publishers, 1968).

9. Marilyn Gittell, "Professionalism and Public Participation in Educational Policy-Making: New York City, A Case Study," The Politics of Urban Education, edited by Marilyn Gittell and Alan G. Hevesi (New York: Praeger Publishers, 1969), p. 163.

10. William Greenbaum and Joseph M. Cronin, "School Board Decision-Making: The Education of Children and the Employment of Adults," (mimeographed, Cambridge, Mass.: Harvard Graduate School of Education, 1971), pp. 6-7.

11. Joseph Pois, "The Board and the General Superintendent," Governing Education: A Reader on Politics, Power and Public School Policy (Garden City, N.Y.: Doubleday, Anchor Press, 1969), pp. 429-30.

12. Badi Foster, "Democracy and Change: The Performance of School Board Members," (mimeographed, Cambridge, Mass.: Harvard Graduate School of Education, 1974), p. 54.

13. Ibid., p. 55.

14. Greenbaum and Cronin, op. cit., pp. 4-5.

15. Robert L. Crain and David Street, "School Desegregation and School Decision Making," In The Politics of Urban Education, edited by

Marilyn Gittell and Alan G. Hevesi (New York: Praeger Publishers, 1969), p. 111.

16. Ibid., p. 110.

17. Ibid., p. 119.

18. "Educators Discuss Board-Superintendent Relations in District," District of Columbia Citizens for Better Public Education Bulletin Board, December 1974, p. 5.

19. Ibid., p. 5.

20. Robert F. Lyke, "Representation and Urban School Boards," in Community Control of Schools, edited by Henry M. Levin (New York: Clarion, 1970), p. 158.

21. Myron Lieberman, "Negotiations: Past, Present, and Future," School Management, May 1973, p. 16.

22. Frederick R. Livingston, "Collective Bargaining and the School Board," in Public Workers and Public Unions, edited by Sam Zagoria, (Englewood Cliffs, N.J.: Prentice-Hall, 1972), p. 74.

23. Ibid., pp. 73-74.

24. Government Employee Relations Report, (Washington, D.C.: Bureau of National Affairs, November 25, 1974), p. B-19.

25. John H. Leddy, "Negotiating with School Teachers: Anatomy of a Muddle," Ohio State Law Journal 33 (1972): 822.

26. Interview with Leslie Jones, Special Assistant for Labor Relations to the Mayor of the District of Columbia, Washington, D.C., October 4, 1974.

27. Interview with Dr. Cornelius Golightly, President of the Detroit Board of Education, Detroit, Mich., June 20, 1974.

28. Clyde W. Summers, "Public Employee Bargaining: A Political Perspective," Yale Law Journal 83 (May 1974): 1164.

29. Joseph M. Cronin, The Control of Urban Schools: Perspective on the Power of Educational Reformers (New York: The Free Press, 1973), pp. 242-44.

30. Government Employee Relations Report (Washington, D.C.: Bureau of National Affairs, July 1, 1974), p. B-15.

31. William R. Hazard, "Courts in the Saddle: School Boards Out," Phi Delta Kappan, December 1974, p. 261.

32. Paul Tractenberg, quoted in "Philadelphia Parents Fight Union Influence Over School Board," Education Daily, January 29, 1975, p. 3.

33. "Philadelphia Parents Fight Union Influence Over School Board," Education Daily, January 29, 1975, p. 3.

34. Harry H. Wellington and Ralph K. Winter, Jr., The Union and the Cities (Washington, D.C.: The Brookings Institution, 1971).

35. Tractenberg, op. cit., p. 3.

36. Ida Klaus, "The Evolution of a Collective Bargaining Relationship in Public Education: New York City's Changing Seven-Year

History," Michigan Law Review 67 (March 1969): 1033-66.

37. Government Employee Relations Report (Washington, D.C.: Bureau of National Affairs, November 11, 1974), p. B-10.

38. Robert L. Ridgley, "Collective Bargaining and Community Involvement in Education: The Trouble with Negotiations," (mimeographed, Boston: League of Women Voters of Massachusetts, 1974), p. 6.

39. Irving H. Sabghir, The Scope of Bargaining in Public Sector Collective Bargaining (Albany: New York State Public Employment Relations Board, 1970), p. 115.

40. Kurt L. Hanslowe and Walter E. Oberer, "Determining the Scope of Negotiations under Public Employment Relations Statutes," Industrial and Labor Relations Review 24 (April 1971): 432-41.

41. Grant F. Shipley, "Determining the Scope of Bargaining under the Indiana Education Employment Relations Act," Indiana Law Journal 49 (Spring 1974): 460-81.

42. Paul Prasow, et al., Scope of Bargaining in the Public Sector: Concepts and Problems (Washington, D.C.: U.S. Department of Labor, 1972), p. 23.

43. Arvid Anderson, "School Policy and Collective Bargaining," mimeographed (Madison: University of Wisconsin, 1973), p. 21.

5

THE RISE OF COMMUNITY PARTICIPATION AND COMMUNITY CONTROL: CONFLICT BETWEEN UNION AND COMMUNITY

Black people in American cities are in the process of developing the power to assume control of these public and private institutions in our community. The single institution which carries the heaviest responsibility for dispensing or promulgating those values which identify a group's consciousness of itself is the educational system. To leave the education of black children in the hands of people who are white and who are racist is tantamount to suicide. *

It is pertinent to recall that the drive for teacher rights, translated into the cry for "teacher power," came at the height of the civil rights movement in the 1960s. It was a time when the Student Nonviolent Coordinating Committee (SNCC) was calling for participatory democracy; it was not long before blacks and the other minorities active in the civil rights movement began to focus on the inferior quality of the educational programs being provided to black youth. Thus, while teachers were seeking to drastically alter the power balance in the educational structure, they found community groups, for the most part black and Spanish-speaking, demanding more of a voice in the operation of schools. Such a situation had the makings of a natural alliance between two historically powerless groups struggling for more control over their own destiny, but the drastic and racially explosive UFT-led strike on Ocean Hill-Brownsville brought an abrupt end to any hope of such an alliance. This chapter examines the evolution of the community

---

*Five State Organizing Committee for Community Control, "A Position Statement" (mimeographed, Cambridge, Mass., January 25, 1968), p. 1.

control movement and in particular explores the sources of conflict
between the people active in this movement and the urban teacher unions. It is necessary to understand these developments in order to
address the larger question of why community groups are now protest-
ing the bargaining structure and what kinds of alternatives are possible. *

Charles V. Hamilton and Stokely Carmichael, in their book Black
Power and the Politics of Liberation in America, say that in order for
society to rid itself of racism a process of political modernization must
occur. Their idea of political modernization embraces three types of
reform: (1) questioning the old values and institutions of the society;
(2) searching for new and different forms of political structure to solve
political and economic problems; and (3) broadening the base of political participation to include more people in the decision-making process.[1] Similarly, Kenneth W. Haskins, an advocate of community

---

*The drive for community control of schools has been extensively
treated in the literature of the last several years. For a descriptive
study of decentralization see Mario Fantini and Marilyn Gittell, Decentralization: Achieving Reform (New York: Praeger Publishers, 1973);
Henry Levin, ed., Community Control of Schools (New York: Clarion,
1970); Annette T. Rubinstein, ed., Schools Against Children: The Case
for Community Control (New York: Monthly Review Press, 1970). For
analyses of Ocean Hill-Brownsville see Maurice R. Berube and Marilyn
Gittell, Confrontation at Ocean Hill-Brownsville (New York: Praeger
Publishers, 1969); Melvin I. Urofsky, ed., Why Teachers Strike:
Teachers' Rights and Community Control (Garden City, N.Y.: Double-
day, Anchor Press, 1970); Joseph Featherstone, Community Control
of Schools, New Republic, January 13, 1968. A series of articles by
Joseph Featherstone, New Republic, 1968. For more general discus-
sions of community control see Charles V. Hamilton and Stokely Car-
michael, Black Power and the Politics of Liberation in America (New
York: Vintage, 1967); also see Hamilton's article "Race and Education:
A Search for Legitimacy," Reprint Series No. 3, Harvard Educational
Review, 1969, pp. 47-62; Kenneth W. Haskins, "A Black Perspective
on Community Control," in Inequality in Education, Center for Law and
Education, Harvard University, November 1973, pp. 23-34; William
Ryan, Blaming the Victim (New York: Vintage, 1972), particularly
Chapter 2. For a comprehensive annotated bibliography on citizen par-
ticipation in schools see Citizen Participation in Education (New Haven:
Institute for Responsive Education, 1974); finally, see Gracie Lee
Boggs, "Education: The Great Obsession," in Education and Black
Struggle: Notes from the Colonized World, a special issue of the Har-
vard Educational Review, 1974, pp. 61-81.

control and a former principal in a community-controlled school in
Washington, D.C., states as follows:

> What is being attacked is not only the total institution,
> but the very reason for its existence. All aspects come
> under scrutiny as the movement for involvement logically
> reaches demand for control. It is impossible to make
> necessary changes to meet the needs of oppressed groups
> without a change in power relationships. [2]

Others also have begun to question the legitimacy of public schools.
Public Education, for instance, came under severe attack because it
represented an institution of which the abject failure was readily visible.
Indeed, a number of prominent white social-science researchers documented the failure of the schools, the Coleman Report being the most
notable. Writers and former teachers, such as Herbert Kohl, Jonathan
Kozol, John Holt, Terry Herndon, and Preston Wilcox, also added fuel
to the flames by writing about the generally authoritarian policies, op-
pressive conditions, and racist nature of public schooling in large urban communities. This crisis of legitimacy became more pronounced
as more attention was given to the failure of nonwhite children in four
areas: reading achievement, rate of progress K-12; incidence of academic versus vocational diplomas among high school graduates; and rate
of college entrance. * Black parents became more concerned about
school systems that were essentially turning out functional illiterates.

Michael B. Katz characterized the schools as building defensive
walls, as follows:

> They have developed organizational structures that moved
> them ever further away from interaction with the commu-
> nities they served, and . . . they even refused to accept
> responsibility for educating anybody successfully in any-
> thing. Once granted a captive audience, they have little
> need to succeed; it has been easier to develop a battery of

---

*Doxey A. Wilkerson takes up these four points in his analysis of
New York City schools in "The Failure of Schools Serving the Black and
Puerto Rican Poor," in Schools against Children, (New York: Monthly
Review Press, 1970), pp. 93-126. Wilkerson's piece, while restricted
to New York City, is symbolic of the overall picture of public school-
ing for third-world children in this country. Also see Report of the
National Advisory Commission on Civil Disorders (New York: Bantam
Books, 1968), particularly the sections dealing with education.

excuses that place the blame for educational failure outside the school and on the home. [3]

Raising a similar issue, Ronald R. Edmonds, Director, Center for
Urban Studies, Harvard Graduate School of Education, expresses a
view shared by many community control advocates:*

> In instances in which the community to be served is eth-
> nically, racially, culturally or economically different
> from the middle-class milieu that characterizes teachers
> and schools, teachers cannot rely on their intuitive under-
> standing of the community to know how best to proceed
> when the purpose is pupil progress that is both acceptable
> to, and appreciated by, the community. Such a circum-
> stance requires school personnel to make parents and
> community representatives instrumental in determining
> the programs and instructional activities of the school.
> The community must be chiefly responsible for the
> school's perception of which bodies of knowledge and
> sets of skills will best prepare students to be of service
> to the community. [4]

The major point of emphasis here is that black parents in cities
became "fed up" with schools that failed to provide any appreciable
learning skills for countless thousands of youngsters. This intense
interest in what was happening to student minds soon became translated
into demands that the professional staff be held accountable, particularly classroom teachers.

Community control extended beyond these issues. Of equal concern was the essence of the educational institution itself and the type
of political control over that institution. The above-mentioned remarks
by Haskins, Hamilton, and Carmichael speak to these issues. By contrast, during the early 1960s the civil rights movement had confined
itself to equal-opportunity issues. The mammoth 1963 March on Washington symbolized these goals, but the intent of the March, as mani-
fested in Martin Luther King's "I Have a Dream" speech, was to obtain
equality within the framework of the existing institutions. The community control movement later challenged these assumptions. Striking
at the core of the educational system's historic values was of prime

---

*For a more detailed account of Edmond's idea on what schools
ought to minimally provide, see "Minimum and Maximums: A Theory
and Design of Social Service Reform," (mimeographed, Cambridge,
Mass.: Center for Urban Studies, Harvard University, April 16, 1974).

importance, since it exposed one aspect of racial exploitation, as follows:

> Certain segments of the white community in this country have always been preoccupied with the education of Black people. Southern slaveholders clearly indicated the attitudes of the total country. The decision-makers in the North set policy and practice based upon the historical slaveholder attitudes.
>
> The educational system for Black people began when they were captured in Africa and its purpose was to make them slaves. They were to be docile; they were to be obedient; they were to see themselves as inferior; they were to remain helpless and be dependent upon the white community. And in each instance, the opposite goals were applied to the white community. They were to produce the master class. Those whites who would not be masters could nevertheless be used in the "education" of Black people and would derive those psychological and economic rewards that accrue from having an exploited group. These same practices and roles have been institutionalized in our educational system. Any move toward changing education for Black people in America must strike at these relationships to be effective. This move goes beyond the equalizing of facilities or even beyond segregation and desegregation. It must undermine a philosophy and beliefs that have maintained themselves for over 400 years. [5]

Community control clearly was not simply a quest for increasing reading scores, although for many black parents this was of paramount interest. Robert Maynard, in his essay "Black Nationalism and Community Schools," succinctly summed up another dimension of the change of emphasis from integration to control as follows:

> According to the blacks' view of the world, it has become necessary to take over the responsibility for their own education and that of their children, partly because of the hostility they divine in white systems but also because of their new self-involvement and thus, their rush toward self-discovery. [6]

This rush to self-involvement is a prominent feature of community control. As already mentioned, the civil rights movement, following the great March on Washington, began to concentrate on increased participation on the part of blacks in social-service institutions. Civil rights groups began to challenge the very notions of the democratic process. This black struggle also prodded the burgeoning antiwar movement into challenging fundamental premises of governmental operations. It was the black movement that gave birth to the so-called New Left. Joseph M. Cronin has aptly summarized this development as follows:

> The new politics reflects a more general concern for democratization in large-scale organizations and a search for a meaningful kind of participation in a society which has lost the kind of intimacy and community that men (women) need to feel accepted and effective. The more radical social welfare professionals recognize both the need for client control of services and the wall of impersonality erected by independent professions. [7]

In 1974 Marcus Raskin described the heart of what the slogan "participatory democracy" meant to many in the late 1960s when he wrote the following in The New Republic:

> If we are to see democracy as something more than an ideological statement or a cover for oligarchic rule in various institutions of privilege, a way must be found to extend democracy into hitherto closed institutions. [8]

Blacks, based on a consistent historical record, have found the schools to be closed institutions whenever they have sought to meaningfully effect the making of school policy.

Thus far, I have identified two primary reasons for the emergence of community control: the first has been the failure of schools to educate the vast majority of blacks and poor, while the second has been the thrust for black self-determination, which in practice has meant political control over social-service institutions. There is a third underlying reason that has given impetus to community control, which is the outright resistance to integration in Northern urban centers by large sectors of the white community. Indeed, the New York City branch of the American Civil Liberties Union, in its 1968 report on the controversy at Ocean Hill-Brownsville stated, "It is crucial to remember that integration was not abandoned by black parents but by the Board of Education, which consistently failed to deliver on the promise of integrated schools."[9]

There is another notable point to mention on the subject of community control and integration. A number of opponents of community control, including Albert Shanker, current President of the AFT, have always insisted in any public statements that community control means a flat rejection of integration. The UFT, for example, labeled black advocates of community control as black separatists, the clear implication being that such people are un-American, since they subvert the American Dream of assimilation. Aside from its assault on the existing power relationships in public schools, community control struck at the very premise of school integration. Thus a whole school of thought, emanating from the <u>Brown</u> decision and the work of reputable human relations experts and liberal social scientists, came under attack. No longer were blacks willing to accept the notion that black children could effectively learn only by attending school with white children.* No longer were blacks willing to delay improvements in ghetto schools while waiting for white society to open its housing and the doors of its schools. The black disability-deficit theory was being torn asunder by the very people in whose "best interest" the theory was designed. This was not an anti-integration development, as some charged; rather, as Haskins has suggested, community control went beyond equal opportunity and attempted to undermine a racist philosophy that had been nourished for 300 years.

In the end, however, it was the insistence on changing the decision makers that caused the widespread controversy over the issue of community control that clearly posed a serious challenge to the prevailing educational power structure.

> The approach if adopted, would return "power to the people," a popular if somewhat vague slogan except when defined as the power to hire and fire teachers. The new approach in effect reversed the trend to centralization, to decision-making by a small elite group and to reliance for virtually all personnel and policy proposals on a professional school superintendent's staff.[10]

---

*Integration as a means to achieve educational equity has continued to be challenged since the formative stages of community control. The following articles provide an analysis by those who questioned the educational premise of school integration: Ronald Edmonds, "A Discussion of Factors to be Considered in Evaluating Desegregation Proposals," (Lansing: Michigan State Department of Education, February 1972); Ronald Edmonds, "Advocating Inequity: A Critique of the Civil Rights Attorney in Class Action Desegregation Suits," <u>The Black Law Journal</u> 3 (1974): 176-83; Derrick Bell, "School Desegregation: Constitutional Right or Obsolete Strategy," (Cambridge, Mass.: Center for Urban Studies, Harvard University, May 16, 1974), mimeographed; Ronald Edmonds, "Critique of Present Desegregation Phase in Boston Schools," Freedom House, Roxbury, February 1975.

Finally, this 1969 statement by the New Urban League in Boston provides an insightful summary of what the overall intent of the national community control movement meant for urban schools:

> Community organizations must be set up with a cross section of people from the black community—parents, professionals, teachers, ministers and interested persons who live in the community. These organizations must move to gain total control over the operation of the schools, including expenditure of monies. The money should be banked in a community bank with local people serving as treasurers and in charge of bookkeeping. The city and state should be made to allot money on a school-by-school basis with each community organization for respective schools determining how the money should be spent. These school-community organizations must also have control over principal and teacher accountability, that is, the power to hire and fire school officials. These school-community organizations must have the power to be involved in the plans for building and rehabilitation of the schools. Construction contracts should be given to black companies. This is community control![11]

THE CLASH BETWEEN THE COMMUNITY AND THE UNION

With the rise of community control then, two new forces were emerging almost simultaneously to challenge the status quo in public education. On the one hand, black parents were demanding both a voice in governance and significant improvements in pupil performance, while on the other, teachers unions were also pressing for an effective voice in school governance. Both forces were largely urban-based. The teachers unions, particularly in the 1960s, won several successful organizing campaigns in major urban centers, in New York; Detroit; Washington, D.C.; Cleveland; Boston; Pittsburgh; Philadelphia; and Newark. In the beginning both groups lashed out at the old professionals and the administrative bureaucracy, and in many instances alliances were formed between teachers unions and black parent groups. Many of these same parents openly supported and campaigned for higher teacher salaries. These two forces were further supported by a leading number of scholars and school critics, who saw nothing but inertia and racism at the top of the school hierarchy. Such a situation had the making of what some described as a natural alliance, but as Joseph Featherstone pointed out, there soon followed the "tragedy" of the disintegration of the alliance over the Ocean Hill-Brownsville clash. [12] How did this happen? While other works cited earlier deal comprehensively with the subject, here I am chiefly concerned with a few important factors that led the new professional union leaders to break the alliance. Donald H. Wollett has provided an insightful statement that tends to strike at the center of the conflict that continues to erupt between teachers unions and community groups:

> The assertions by organized groups of parents—whether
> in Scarsdale or in Ocean Hill-Brownsville—that the neigh-
> borhood public schools are "theirs" and that they must
> have total control over who is hired, what they teach and
> what methods they use are squarely opposed to the high-
> est aspirations of public teachers. [13]

Continuing, he stresses the concept of teacher self-determination and the teachers' role as alleged experts:

> The pressure for community control being applied by the
> leadership of racial and ethnic groups in the affected
> neighborhood merely compounds the conflict. If teach-
> ing is truly a profession teachers must be recognized
> as having a special competence to help define the stand-
> ards of their practice and the quality of service provided
> to their clientele. [14]

Like many of the teachers unions, Wollett does not relate community control to racist institutions and the virtual exclusion of black citizens from decision-making positions: the struggle over control in Scarsdale can hardly be equated with the struggle in the poverty-ridden community of Ocean Hill-Brownsville. However, this is another matter; what is of import here is Wollett's strong suggestion that there is an inevitable conflict between parents demanding control over "their" schools and the "highest aspirations of teachers." Extending this logic, it would seem that instead of the old professionals making all the important decisions, the new professionals should simply replace the old educational power structure through bargaining.

As Mario Fantini states, "simplistic demands [made by parents] lead many professionals to be skeptical of the right of parents to participate because of their lack of technical qualifications to engage in educational decisions." [15] Hence one engages in a dangerous "romance with the Left" if any demand made by oppressed parents is deemed worthy of support. Fantini goes on to say, "However the question is actually not whether parents now know how, but what they can come to know through involvement and through open access to educational information."[16] However, once the union secured a power base, its attitude toward parent involvement took a new direction.

Another reason for the unions' change in stance toward community involvement was that once they had become central powers many urban unions were basically content to ally themselves with the existing power structure they had so long fought. This is not to say that the unions ceased their criticism of the school bureaucracy, but now the unions waged their fight as one of the parties within the school structure. They had carved out a part of the stale pie, and sharing this newly-won power with community groups was seen as a threat to union power. Simply put, the union, which had just recently won political status, was evidently unwilling to relinquish these new political gains to groups of parents who were outside the educational structure.

Equally important is the fact that the union leadership, as well as the board's chief negotiator, preferred a centralized bargaining structure. Negotiating from the top meant not only that power was concentrated at this level, but also that it would be much easier for the union staff to operate because the central union maintained structural control in two broad and significant areas: (1) day-to-day relations with the school administration and (2) staff dominance over the union itself. The rank-and-file came to rely on the union power "downtown," a concept promoted by union leaders. In the early stages of bargaining, centralization of negotiation is essential to establish a united front and avoid inequities, but at a later stage this same centralization can lead to a displacement of goals and to vested interests on the part of the leadership. This centralization also was supported by the school administrations' negotiating offices. This latter point is often neglected by critics of the unions today, although they quickly and often accurately point out that the unions have embraced the status quo, as does Fantini, as follows:

> The UFT, AFT, NEA have won battles that improve their power with the existing system, not a reformed one. Together, they are now the most powerful groups controlling a public school system that is centralized, monolithic and uniform. They are winning and their prize is the standard system. Teachers' organizations now prefer a centralized structure. [17]

To a large degree, such criticism is a distortion of politics in education today. Teachers unions are a significant force and becoming more so in educational politics, but it is extremely questionable whether they are "the most powerful groups controlling a public school system." Negotiated agreements, and the current inability of powerful urban teachers unions to prevent teacher layoffs, reveal that unions are simply not all-powerful. On the other hand it is true that teacher unions have come to embrace the prevailing school structure, much as the industrial unions have come to accept the underlying principles of a capitalistic economic system.

Acceptance of acting within the status quo is revealed by the latest position taken by one of the most progressive teachers unions in the country, the Washington Teachers Union in Washington, D.C.* In its nascent stage of development, the WTU worked for community participation in the schools and sought to alter the relationship between a centralized union and the school administration. Under the new superintendency of Barbara Sizemore, a plan to decentralize the Washington schools was submitted and is now being implemented. Much of the plan can and should legitimately be questioned. In fact, not surprisingly, the centralized school board has itself resisted such a move to decentralize the schools.

Nevertheless, the union, instead of playing a constructive role by working for the best method of achieving this plan, a type of behavior that would be consistent with its support of community control and teacher rank-and-file participation, has raised questions of "who is responsible for the running of the school system." In the January 1975 issue of the Washington Teacher, the union called for the resignation of Superintendent Sizemore, citing several specific reasons, some of which indicate that the union wishes no alteration in the school structure, regardless of who holds the superintendency. The pertinent section of the union complaint follows:

> Perhaps the most significant reason for a change is that cultivation of an appearance of shared power has led to such confusion and diffusion of responsibility that blame cannot be fixed when things go wrong. The thinking behind PACTS, for example, seems to be that if local schools are kept busy dealing with minutiae they will have little time or incentive to keep track of goings-on in the upper echelons of administration. [PACTS is discussed further in the next chapter.]

*Like many urban teachers unions at their formative stages, the WTU took a number of progressive positions. In many instances, the WTU was even more progressive than most teachers unions. Among some of the progressive stances taken by the WTU in its early years were its support for community control; its support for a public school to be run by teachers and parents without union or administration intervention; support for teacher peer evaluation; and support for a student rights bill.

> The concept of the administrative team is an-
> ther device for diluting responsibility; it brings to-
> gether several people who will arrive at a consensus
> solution to a problem.
>
> The results have shown that, after discussion,
> agreement is reached at the lowest common denom-
> inator; that is reported as the consensus, and there
> is no provision made for a minority report. Dissent
> is stifled through fear, although few team members
> will admit it and most prefer to say they will go along
> with the majority out of a sense of loyalty. Whatever
> the reason given, the net result is the same: A medi-
> ocre report is given, and no one is responsible.
>
> Decentralization has produced a similar effect.
> A policy is announced, but there is no enforcing of
> the policy by a responsible authority. The result is
> total confusion, disarray, and demoralization. Who
> is responsible?
>
> The Union's contention is that the chief admin-
> istrator of the school system is responsible. [18]

The WTU has every right to be concerned about the drift of the
school system, as well as about any reorganizational plan. My major
point, however, is that this latest stance simply demonstrates that
teachers union leaders will now fight determinedly to preserve a mono-
lithic school structure.* Surprisingly, in the same article the union
boasts that it sat by for a year as a passive observer of the superintendent's actions. This hardly reveals a progressive union advocating
positive alterations in the status quo.

This move by teachers unions to opt for mere consolidation of
their own power within the existing system has placed a monumental
barrier in the path of parents who seek to change the balance of the
school power structure. In effect the unions have become part and
parcel of the same clique of educators, in a centralized school system
endeavoring to maintain its power.

———————————

*While critical of the WTU's position here, I should indicate that
as of February 1975 the controversy over the WTU contract had again
demonstrated that unions are not by any means exercising dominant
control. On February 5, 1975, for instance, the District of Columbia
Board of Education voted to abrogate the current bargaining agreement,
including the grievance and arbitration procedures, and also to cancel
the provisions for dues deductions, this last item being the economic
lifeline of the union. In many quarters this was viewed as a "union
busting" tactic.

UNION-COMMUNITY ALLIANCES: SOME EXCEPTIONS

It would be misleading, however, to give the impression that no union group has been willing to share decision-making power over educational policies with the community. At the 1968 AFT convention in Cleveland, just prior to the Ocean Hill-Brownsville strike, the New Caucus, an opposition caucus to the AFT leadership, issued a position paper in full support of community control. Focusing on decision making, the caucus declared as follows:

> Frustrated by the failure of their efforts, the commu-
> nity changed the focus of the struggle. If the decision-
> makers are not responsive to the needs of the children
> they are charged with educating, why not change the
> decision-makers? Why not put the decisions in the
> hands of those with the greatest stake in the achieve-
> ment of the children, their parent and local commu-
> nity leadership? The concept is, after all, not revo-
> lutionary. It is not only rooted in the genesis of Amer-
> ican public education, but it is also the present reality
> for Americans living outside the large urban areas.
> It will not erode the present power of those living in
> the so-called "good" school districts of the city to
> continue to control their own schools; it will simply
> give the same rights to those presently without power
> to influence decisions that may determine the very
> direction of their children's lives.[19]

Continuing, the statement emphasized the necessity for professionals to work with the community, and it indicated what alternative would be left to the community if black and Puerto Rican parents and urban unions could not forge a working alliance.

> The Union will continue to exist, and will continue
> to be responsible for the protection of teachers'
> rights. The people who are advocating these new
> changes are, many of them, the same people who
> helped the teachers win the right to union represen-
> tation. They will only oppose teacher unionism when
> it thwarts their own legitimate goals. Furthermore,
> people whose major concern is the education of their
> children will inevitably respond to, respect and pro-
> tect the teacher who demonstrates a willingness to
> do the best possible job for the children.

> The greatest danger to the teacher and the union
> is the chaos that results from the unwillingness of the
> school system to change, leaving those who see the
> change as necessary and inevitable no alternative but
> to disrupt and destroy. A union that fights necessary
> and desirable change—that opposes the legitimate aims
> of the parents and community they purport to serve—
> that isolates itself from the forward-looking groups
> and organizations concerned with educational progress,
> only contributes to chaos and does a disservice to its
> membership and the labor movement as a whole. It
> threatens the very viability and unity of the union it-
> self.[20]

Further, in New York City a group of UFT members, a tiny
minority of the membership to be sure, circulated a pamphlet that
urged teachers to work for community control, stressing that there
did not necessarily have to be a conflict between the rights of organized
teachers and the demands of poor parents seeking accountability and
a measure of influence in the running of schools.[21]

These voices did not hold sway either in the AFT or the NEA, nor
in most large urban centers. Such positions were rejected out of hand,
leaving union leaders to form both formal and informal alliances with
the old professionals in the school system, against those citizens who
had been consistently and systematically excluded from any substantive
role in making decisions affecting the education of their children. On
this point, the New Caucus clearly pinpointed one form of racism that
had left its imprint on the schools, as follows:

> What has happened in New York parallels what has
> taken place in urban centers everywhere. The pupil
> population has become more than half Negro and Puer-
> to Rican—while the Board of Education and profession-
> al staff are still dominated by and reflect the interests
> and concerns of the white middle class. It is this so-
> cial, economic and cultural distance between those
> who make the decisions and those who are affected
> by them that is at the root of much of the present
> controversy.[22]

Taking into account this observation and the earlier remarks of
Haskins, it is clear that underlying much of the clash over the balance
of power in urban schools has been the enduring legacy of the African
slave trade.* In many respects community control once again only

---

*An excellent brief account tracing the rise of racism in America
can be found in Jack O'Dell's "Foundations of Racism in American

served to highlight the prophetic words of W. E. B. DuBois when he said, "The problem of the twentieth century is the problem of the color line."[23]

PARENT PARTICIPATION AND THE
SCOPE OF NEGOTIATIONS

The clash in Ocean Hill-Brownsville between the UFT and the black community was certainly the most dramatic break between old allies. The once powerless union, which only a few years before had been a struggling organization fighting for its own survival, had become a power in its own right and was now resisting the efforts of the black urban poor, who were seeking equality of educational opportunity for their young as well as a degree of control over a critical institution in society.

What occurred in New York City, however, had ripple effects across the country. Other unions became very wary of pending decentralization plans. As Cronin has pointed out, the Detroit decentralization plan, for instance, would most likely not have passed the Michigan legislature if the Detroit Federation of Teachers had lost its right to bargain an overall agreement covering the decentralized school districts.[24] In New York City, a committee report of the New York Bar Association has made crystal clear the implications of labor negotiations and the transfer of power to local school boards under New York's decentralization act: "The legislature did not vest in the community boards the most significant aspect of labor relations: the negotiations of a contract."[25] Negotiations were kept centralized, just as in Detroit; in fact, in all urban centers in which teachers are represented by the union, bargaining is limited to one master agreement covering all teachers.

Community control must also be placed in the context of the widening of the scope of negotiations. While unions were gaining a foothold in the educational power structure and making headway into many policy areas, parent and community groups, who were sealed off both from the bargaining structure and from any meaningful access to boards of education, now became even more concerned with what was being negotiated at the bargaining table. The earlier-mentioned suit by the Education Law Center is a prime example of this concern.

Life," Freedomways 4 (Fall 1964). Also see Charles W. Cheng, "The My Lai Tradition in the Development of the American Capitalist State: The Death Hunt of American Indians and the Rise of Racism," (mimeographed, Antioch College, January 1972).

Even the League of Women Voters of Massachusetts, an essentially white upper-middle-class organization, has taken up the issue.* The League, for instance, drafted a collective bargaining survey in January 1975 and circulated it in all the school districts in Massachusetts. (See Appendix.) Among some of the questions asked are the following:

How is collective bargaining conducted in your district? (Closed session or open public session?)
If not open public sessions, are the bargaining proposals available to the public during negotiations? If so, how?
Does the school committee inform the public of their general goals before the negotiations begin? Do they make interim reports? Do they make public the terms of the contract after it is signed? If so, what methods of informing the public are used?
Do you think that the public should be involved in negotiations? If not, for what reasons? If so, how?
Which of the following issues are included within the scope of bargaining in your district?
salaries___school hours___determining class size___ student discipline policies or practices___curriculum ___placement of handicapped children___evaluation of teacher performance___selection of textbooks___ tenure rules and regulations___ .
Does your school district have a policy manual? Is there anything in the policy manual that relates to collective bargaining? If so, what are the areas covered?
Specifically, how are the interests of students being represented at the bargaining tables?[26]

A 1975 report entitled "The Community at the Bargaining Table," prepared by a study team of the Institute for Responsive Education, also tends to underline the increasing interest shown by groups that do not directly participate in the bargaining process.[27] Oddly enough, the New York City Bar Association report touches on a refrain often articulated by teachers unions leaders, who have maintained that anything to do with the operating of schools was set up for negotiations. The report gives another perspective to this union notion by asserting that

---

*On April 12, 1975, an all-day conference on the community at the bargaining table was sponsored by the League of Women Voters in conjunction with the Institute for Responsive Education and the School of Education at Boston University.

where local community boards are involved "there is nothing that goes on in collective negotiations regarding those schools that does not affect their interests."[28]

The report by the Institute for Responsive Education is emphatic in its support of the right of teachers to organize and collectively bargain to promote their legitimate interests in the educational process.[29] Parents, on the other hand, also have legitimate educational interests. Ideally parents and teachers ought to be working in harmony with one another; the pitting of teachers and parents against one another can only lead to further disastrous results for poor and minority students. Nevertheless, if the legitimate interests of poor parents are thwarted by the bargaining structure, then these groups may resort to "union-busting tactics" as a desperate measure. Union busting is no solution, since any such move implicitly contains a strong antiteacher sentiment. Reversing educational history by opposing the organizing of teachers would be both counterproductive and politically reactionary: actions like the parents union suit in Philadelphia, for instance, while obviously revealing that the parents perceive their interests to be ignored in negotiations, give credence to antiunion forces and in the end will only serve to aggravate parent-teacher conflict.

However, the fact remains that with the growth of bargaining, these new classes of professionals have emerged to become the dominant decision makers within the public-education power structure. To repeat, even if a large urban school board is considered to be a representative board on which the poor and the minorities have gained political standing, the bargaining structure, as I have indicated, precludes any substantial contribution to the end results of negotiations by the board itself. Ratification of the contract by the board is more a sign of participation in the technical procedure than of substantive participation. This is particularly evident when the role of the three new professional classes described in Chapter 4 is taken into account.

Given this situation, there are at least two courses of action that can be comtemplated, one dealing with the bargaining structure and the other dealing with the general character of teachers unions. The second alternative will be treated in the final chapter of this book. The first alternative, which is to find constructive ways to bridge the gap between the teachers unions and the community groups that are demanding a stronger voice in educational decision making within the present framework of the bargaining process, is the subject of the next chapter. Are there alternatives that can enhance both teacher rank-and-file and parent participation in the running of our schools, that will ultimately lead to greater community participation and control over social service institutions? Can we, as Grace Lee Boggs once asked, "educate to govern?" As she wrote in 1974,

the situation since Watergate provides those who care
about the future of this country with an unparalleled
opportunity to challenge all Americans to take this
giant step—to seek a new concept of active citizenship
and of self-government, of governement by the people
and of the people which is far more advanced than
the concept for the people under which we have been
living.[30]

NOTES

1. Charles V. Hamilton and Stokely Carmichael, Black Power
and the Politics of Liberation in America, (New York: Vintage, 1967),
p. 39.

2. Kenneth W. Haskins, "A Black Perspective on Community
Control," Inequality in Education, Center for Law and Education, Harvard University, November 1973, p. 29.

3. Michael B. Katz, Class, Bureaucracy and Schools: The Illusion of Educational Change in America (New York: Praeger Publishers,
1971), p. 113.

4. Ronald R. Edmonds, "Minimum and Maximums: A Theory and
Design of Social Service Reform," (mimeographed, Cambridge, Mass.:
Center for Urban Studies, Harvard University, April 16, 1974), p. 10.

5. Haskins, op. cit., p. 24.

6. Robert C. Maynard, "Black Nationalism and Community
Schools," in Community Control of Schools, edited by Henry Levin
(New York: Clarion, 1969), p. 111.

7. Joseph M. Cronin, The Control of Urban Schools: Perspective on the Power of Educational Reformers (New York: The Free
Press, 1973), p. 224.

8. Marcus G. Raskin, "Ersatz Democracy and the Real Thing,"
The New Republic, November 9, 1974, p. 28.

9. "The Burden of Blame: A Report on the Ocean Hill-Brownsville School Controversy," New York American Civil Liberties Union,
New York, October 9, 1968, p. 3.

10. Cronin, op. cit., p. 183.

11. Ibid., p. 186.

12. Joseph Featherstone, "Community Control of Our Schools,"
The New Republic, January 13, 1968, p. 18.

13. Donald H. Wollett, "The Coming Revolution in Public School
Management," Michigan Law Review 67 (March 1969): 1017-32.

14. Ibid., p. 1031.

15. Mario Fantini, What's Best for Children: Resolving the Power Struggle Between Parents and Teachers (New York: Anchor Press, 1974), pp. 19-20.

16. Ibid., p. 20.

17. Ibid., p. 96.

18. "Time for a Change," Washington, D.C., Teacher, January 1975, pp. 1-3.

19. "Community Control and the Future of the AFT," a position paper by the New Caucus, American Federation of Teachers Annual Convention, Cleveland, Ohio, August 1968, p. 2.

20. Ibid., p. 4.

21. "Community Control Is Community Responsibility," (pamphlet, New York: Coalition for Community Control, 1968).

22. "Community Control and the Future of the AFT," op. cit., p. 4.

23. W. E. B. DuBois, The Souls of Black Folk (New York: Crest Books, 1961), p. 23.

24. Cronin, op. cit., p. 198.

25. The Association of the Bar of the City of New York, The Committee on Municipal Affairs and the Committee on Labor and Social Security Legislation, "The New York City School Decentralization Law and Its Effect on Collective Bargaining," May 1972, p. 1.

26. League of Women Voters of Massachusetts, "Survey on Collective Bargaining in Local School Districts," Boston: League of Women Voters, January 1975.

27. Seymour Sarason, Charles Cheng, and Don Davies, "The Community at the Bargaining Table," report to the Institute for Responsive Education, Boston, Mass., 1975.

28. The Association of the Bar of the City of New York, op.cit., p. 4.

29. Sarason, op. cit., p. 1.

30. Grace Lee Boggs, "The Search for Human Identity in America," (mimeographed, New Haven, Conn.: Yale College, 1974), p. 4.

6

> The goal of such restructuring is to ensure that one parti-
> cular interest group, the public employee union, does not
> gain a substantial competitive advantage over other interest
> groups in pursuing its claim on government. The point is
> not that there now exists some perfect balance among in-
> terest groups that must not be disturbed, but simply that it
> is a mistake to institutionalize through law, techniques that
> have the promise of giving one group disproportional power.*

The new technostructure, consisting of union staff, third-party
neutrals and board negotiators, occupies a critical position in public
education, as indicated in Chapter 4. These parties have catapulted to
prominence in school politics as a direct result of the campaign by
teachers to secure collective bargaining. With the expansion of the
scope of bargaining, a number of people began to inquire whether the
collective bargaining model of the private sector is completely applicable to the public sector. This issue has become the most pronounced
in teacher bargaining. Harry H. Wellington and Ralph K. Winter, Jr.,
as noted earlier, have questioned the legitimacy of the bargaining structure itself, arguing that the widening of scope meant unions were gaining an unfair political advantage over other interest groups in the making of public policy. Furthermore, as we have seen, it is not only scholars who have become interested in the bargaining structure. Urban
community groups, especially with the expansion of scope and the

---

*Harry H. Wellington and Ralph K. Winter, Jr., The Unions and
the Cities (Washington, D.C.: The Brookings Institution, 1971), p. 49.

setback for community control, have also begun to protest their "disenfranchised" status and to challenge the current bargaining structure.

COMMUNITY PARTICIPATION
IN THE BARGAINING STRUCTURE

Wholesale destruction of the existing bargaining structure clearly
is not a logical approach to changing the situation. An effort to eliminate bargaining would undoubtedly lead to a severe labor confrontation
that could only create animosity between teachers and parents; yet as
indicated at the outset, serious attention must be given to exploring
ways in which the bargaining process may be altered to include citizens
who are now excluded from any form of direct participation in negotiations. This chapter will concentrate on proposing alternatives to the
present bargaining practices. In some cases, the suggested proposals
represent mild reforms, while in a few others the suggestions could
result in a radical departure from the present adversary form of collective bargaining.

First, an overall summary of findings from interviews conducted
for this study will be given. Second, some specific examples will be
cited of cases in which the community participates in teacher negotiations. Third, some hypothetical alternatives not yet tested in public
education will be discussed. Inherent in the discussion of community
participation in the bargaining process is the value judgement that
those who will be affected by decisions should participate in the decision-making process; that is, there should be "meaningful representation." Seymour Sarason has said that meaningful representation in bargaining would mean that (1) the board and union would know before collective bargaining begins precisely what issues community groups wish
to have on the table; (2) the community groups would be given some idea
of the priorities the union and board had established for themselves;
and (3) the community groups would be informed of the implications of
agreements.[1] I would add another criterion to those Sarason cites:
Community groups should be afforded some concrete way to participate
in the actual negotiation procedures once bargaining has begun.

To examine the feasibility of altering the bargaining structure,
I interviewed a number of prominent people involved in teacher collective bargaining.* The purpose of the interviews was to ascertain from

---

*This section of the study will report on the 30 interviews I per-
sonally conducted during the course of the study. Furthermore, as a
member of the Institute of Responsive Education team that issued the
booklet The Community at the Bargaining Table in January 1975, I

these individuals their views on two central issues: (1) how they perceive the present teacher bargaining structure in the context of the
representation of diverse community interests as the scope of negotiations widens and (2) how they would view direct community participation in the negotiating process. Among some of the people interviewed
were national AFT and NEA leaders, local teacher union leaders,
board members, negotiators for boards of education, arbitrators and
mediators, and parents.

Nearly all the interviewees supported the right of the community
to influence school policies and practices. However, many of the respondents were opposed to allowing the community to become directly
involved in the collective bargaining process. One individual warned
that "having parents and community groups represent themselves would
undermine the democratic foundations on which this country was built."
Others defended the legal right of the school board to be the sole representative of the public in bargaining, but blamed the community for
not exercising its right to elect responsive board members.

A number of respondents believed that even if it were desirable
to include the community in different ways, most citizens would not
be willing to devote the time that would be necessary to understand the
complex matters being negotiated. In a similar vein, many interviewees objected to the lack of expertise that community people would bring
to the sophisticated process of collective bargaining. "This is no game
for amateurs," was a common underlying theme. In addition, there
was strong belief that the interest of parents and others is transitory
and very limited.

Loss of efficiency and stability as a result of community participation was feared by many. Some predicted near-anarchy if ill-inform-
ed and inexperienced community members should be involved directly,
or indirectly, in the bargaining process.

These viewpoints all raise legitimate questions; yet while many
parents would not have the available time, others would; and similarly,
collective bargaining can be viewed as a complex process, but that
does not mean that parents cannot learn about the process through
workshops, forums, and firsthand experience. After all, the

-----

had access to nearly 30 more interviews, handled by two other members of the study team. The results of these interviews are incorporated in this section. A listing of the people I interviewed is found in
the bibliography. Much of the material covered here will be found in
Section II of the Institute of Responsive Education study. Some sections
of the report, which I assisted in writing, have been included verbatim,
although substantive variations in the suggested alternatives occur
throughout.

professional negotiators on both sides of the table were not made but developed, a development born out of practical experience.

One experienced mediator and member of the faculty at the Sloan School at MIT pointed out that community representatives could not be held responsible for the outcome of a negotiated agreement. They would not be obligated on a "day-to-day basis to live with the ramifications of the agreement they helped to negotiate." This viewpoint was shared by the president of the Newark Teachers Union. In effect, both were saying that community people would not be in a position to implement or enforce the agreements they had helped to negotiate; this task would remain with the professionals. Again this is a valid concern. Parents would have to accept responsibility for certain functions of the contract. However, one can easily imagine the parents being held accountable for their participation when new contract provisions might be negotiated concerning such issues as discipline or work on joint committees. Involvement in decision making carries with it a new obligation for all parties. Community participants, for instance, cannot walk away from the bargaining table and say, "Its now up to you to implement." The important point, though, is that this objection should not deter the working out of a responsible relationship among these parties on an ongoing basis.

Interviewees in larger cities expressed the fear that if the community were allowed into the process, its representatives would be the "same old political leaders." There would be no way to insure that those chosen would be "truly representative."

In short, there was not overwhelming support for including the community in the bargaining process in new ways, although there was agreement about the right of the community to determine educational policy.

SCHOOL BOARD RESPONSIVENESS

There was strong agreement, even among some of the school board members, that the boards are not adequately responsive to the concerns and demands of community groups. Those from small towns and suburbs viewed their school boards as being more responsive and representative of the community than did their urban counterparts.

Many respondents attribute the failure of school boards to the rise of a professionalized, bureaucratic technostructure that controls educational decision making and policy development. The underlying theme was the relinquishing of policy-making responsibilities by the lay boards to the professionals. The board members interviewed confirmed the practice of assigning primary responsibility for the collective bargaining process to a full-time professional, often a deputy or

assistant superintendent. Many school systems reported that even if
the deputy or assistant superintendent was not solely responsible for
conducting the negotiations, he still served as the main advisor to a
part-time professional negotiator.

Some perceived their board members as inadequately responsive
to the community simply because educational quality and instructional
matters are not their central concerns. They saw board members as
politicians, using their school board appointments or elections as
steppingstones to other public offices. Other board members were
perceived as businessmen or businesswomen, whose interest in educational quality was secondary to their concern about the tax rate.
More significantly, racism was cited as a cause of unresponsive board
behavior.

SCOPE OF NEGOTIATIONS

Most interviewees had a difficult time making the distinction between "conditions of work" (almost universally seen as a legitimate
area of collective bargaining) and educational policy. This difficulty
of definition often leads to debate and to impasse in the negotiating process. Again their views tended to confirm the problem of scope, as
discussed in Chapter 2.

Strong views were expressed on this matter. One major viewpoint was that working conditions and educational policy are so closely
intertwined that making a distinction between them is not possible.
Those holding this viewpoint see almost any policy, practice, or issue
affecting the schools as a legitimate part of the bargaining process.
At the other end of the spectrum of opinions, there were a few who argued that "working conditions" can, at least in theory, be narrowly
defined. Even such things as class size and pupil discipline policies
may be ruled "out of bounds."

On a practical level, however, most of the interviewees agreed
that the distinctions could not be easily drawn. In practice the areas to
be included are determined by the negotiating parties, with theoretical
definitions and distinctions having little relevance. Nearly everyone
agreed or implied that bargaining has a strong impact on almost all
aspects of educational policy and practice.

There was nearly universal agreement that the scope of negotiations will continue to expand into most areas of educational policy and
practice. Some pointed out that the recent history of labor relations
indicates a steady widening of scope, from salaries and fringe benefits to working conditions, to staff development, to pupil personnel procedures, to textbook selection, to parent-school relations, and to

curriculum. Others stated that education was likely to be affected by current developments in the private sector, where there also is a trend toward a broadening of scope.

The president of the Connecticut Federation of Teachers indicated that the general tightness of the overall economy will force union leaders to focus on educational policy rather than on traditional "bread and butter" issues. One law professor even put forth the notion that since the shortage of teachers has disappeared, the surplus of personnel will eventually lead to reduced salaries, with the teachers unions consequently forced to seek gains in educational policy areas.

EXAMPLES OF COMMUNITY INPUT

Not surprisingly, there seem to be few school districts or teachers organizations that have tried to modify the conventional bilateral collective bargaining procedure; nevertheless, a few examples of efforts to involve the community in the process were discovered.

In 1972 the chief negotiator for the Philadelphia Board of Education invited a group of concerned parents to participate in the negotiations. The parents were given the option of joining either the union or the board team of negotiators. After joining the board's team for the first bargaining session, the parent group chose to disassociate itself and serve as an independent third party at the bargaining table. Following this decision, the board's spokesperson "disinvited" the parents from future sessions. The experience in Philadelphia makes it clear that parents have priorities and concerns that differ from those of either the board or the union. They will not willingly be a part of a bilateral model.* It should be recalled that recently a parents union in Philadelphia filed suit attempting to prohibit the board and union from negotiating over policy matters.

In an effort to avoid the conflict that occurred in Philadelphia, the Detroit Board of Education in 1974 introduced a plan to involve the community indirectly. The plan provides for periodic meetings of 16 community representatives, two from each of the eight regional districts,

---

*In 1972 Edward Simpkins was the chief negotiator for the Philadelphia Board of Education. He was among those interviewed for this study. On the question of parent participation, he now believes that for parents to participate directly in the bargaining process, they should be paid. Such payment, he suggests, could be borne by the union and the board of education. Simpkins still maintains that the parents should be members of either the union or board team.

with a representative of the superintendent's office to discuss the issues and the progress in negotiations. Community representatives are encouraged to comment on both the union and the board positions on any issue.

The shortcomings of this method of community involvement in the negotiating process are already apparent, even though the experiment has just begun. The president of the Board of Education in Detroit expressed doubts about whether this method will allow the community to have meaningful access to the bargaining process. The plan does not allow the community direct or independent access to the decision-making process at the bargaining table. By participating indirectly, the community is highly dependent upon the superintendent's representative for its information and understanding of the process, and this dependency could hinder the community's ability to evaluate and respond directly to the board and the union. At the same time, in this case, this arrangement would allow the school board to use the community for its own political leverage in the negotiations. Underlying this method of involving the community in collective bargaining is the assumption that the community and the board are allies while the community and the union are adversaries. This approach could widen the gap between the community and its teachers—the two groups that most directly affect the learning experience of the children, and the two groups with the most reason to work in an atmosphere of cooperation.

However, the Detroit plan may have some promise, since it does give community representatives a chance to familiarize themselves with the complexities of bargaining and may be a useful first step toward more direct participation. It allows the community limited input into the bargaining discussions. The community may even be able to influence the board's positions and affect the outcome of the negotiations.

In the spring of 1974 the Newark Teachers Union (NTU) and a group of parents from one school successfully negotiated a supplementary agreement on the implementation of a federal program. (See Appendix for a copy of the agreement.) After the agreement was reached, the union and the parent group presented the supplementary contract to the board of education for ratification. The board at first objected, considering such an independent agreement as an attack on its authority, but later it ratified this agreement. As of January 1975, the Union President, Carol Graves, indicated that the agreement was working well. This small effort in Newark is particularly significant in view of the bitter antagonisms that had developed between the teachers union and the community in the 1971 teachers strike. In fact, the parents who negotiated this supplementary contract had opposed the teachers strike. The parents who participated in this effort have proposed that the experiment become a model for additional supplementary agreements with the union. It is noteworthy that while the union has taken a progressive step in negotiating this agreement, it does not favor including the parents in the negotiating of the overall agreement. The parents, however, have expressed a deep interest in becoming involved in the central negotiations.*

In Chicago the central board of education opened bargaining sessions to the public, but after an initial enthusiastic response, most community members stopped attending the formal bargaining sessions. Two factors help to explain this loss of interest: (1) the community members were allowed only as observers and (2) the meetings were often long and tiring.

Open negotiation is not without merit, despite these limitations. Even if limited to the role of observers, the community members can become knowledgeable about the dynamics of the process and can react concretely outside the meetings to board and union positions. Workshops could be developed to enhance community understanding of the negotiations.

In Toledo, Ohio, the teachers union has invloved the community in the initial stages of its negotiations by asking community representatives to assist in the formulation of its demands. Community participation is limited to this initial stage. However, in Montgomery County, Maryland, two parents participate as observers in the actual bargaining sessions. In another large, suburban district, Fairfax County, Virginia, final ratification of the district teachers association contract is postponed for six months while the community is informed and given an opportunity to react.

————————————

*Interestingly, I interviewed the president of the NTU and the parent representatives at the same time in a restaurant near the union office. During our discussion a topic came up which demonstrates a reason why the "secrecy" of negotiations should end. While discussing the history of the relationship between the community and the union, one of the parents pointed out how ridiculous it had been for the union to seek paternal leave for male teachers a few years ago in negotiations. Carol Graves responded by carefully explaining why the male should be present when a newborn child arrives home, and the parents became persuaded that the demand was a legitimate one. Clearly the point to be made is that when the opportunity was afforded, the union had to justify the demand on its own merits. Such openness provides the parents an equal opportunity to question and even alter a demand being put forth. This is not to say that unions and parents will always agree, but that the discussion illustrates that the parties can communicate and possibly act in cooperation in shaping bargaining demands. Currently there are very few instances in which teachers meet with community groups to discuss their bargaining demands or goals.

WASHINGTON, D.C.:
COMMUNITY COUNCILS CONCEPT RESISTED

In my earlier paper, "The Scope of Teacher Negotiations in the Evolutionary Development of the Collective Bargaining Process,"[2] I devoted considerable attention to a new development in Washington, D.C., that seemed to make possible the evolution of a new bargaining structure. I pointed out that the new superintendent, Barbara Sizemore, had announced her intention to establish community councils at each school. These councils were to be known as PACTS, an acronym for "parents, administrators, community representatives, teachers, and students." I further stressed that such a proposal could result in a structural alteration in the bargaining process; hence the formation of PACTS could conceivably lead to a clash between the teachers' bargaining agent, the WTU, and the local PACTS, particularly if PACTS were to have decision-making power. Nevertheless, the possibility of developing a new bargaining structure was distinctly there. This was true for at least two reasons: (1) the union, as stated in Chapter 4, still articulated a progressive image and (2) its president, William Simons, had long supported community control. Barbara Sizemore, herself a supporter of community control, had brought to her administration Kenneth W. Haskins, a community control advocate and a former principal in Morgan Community School in Washington. In short, the leadership of the school administration and the union seemed to have an outlook that would make it more than possible for them to work together in developing a different and potentially dynamic democratic process. This would promote effective participatory decision making by all groups interested in the education of students in the twelfth-largest school system in the nation.

From my interviews with Simons and with Haskins in November 1973, it appeared that PACTS would gain favorable backing from the union. Bargaining was about to begin on the fourth contract, and each party disclosed a willingness to explore the subject of PACTS in the forthcoming contract talks. Unfortunately, the matter was never treated in negotiations; in fact, one of the school organizers for PACTS, Al Gaskins, said it might have been wise to include some provision in the contract related to PACTS. Failure to include discussion of PACTS in negotiations was quite valid from one point of view, since parents and students were excluded from bargaining; it would be a breach of the PACTS concept to negotiate any agreement without these parties participating. However, the substance of PACTS need not have been discussed: a mere recognition of the concept in the bargaining process would have demonstrated a commitment on the part of the board of education and the union to deal with PACTS. This, I believe, was the core

of the problem; neither the union nor the board's chief negotiator wanted
to discuss the issue. PACTS posed too many questions for the technostructure on both sides of the table.

The negotiations, though, represent only one problem area en-
countered by PACTS. During the last year PACTS has experienced
many setbacks. Shortly after negotiations began, the union issued a
statement urging teachers not to cooperate in the forming of PACTS in
each school. The union based its opposition on several factors: (1) the
concept was too vague; (2) it did not hold the superintendent responsible
for running the schools, and (3) the union had had an unsatisfactory experience with PACTS and charged that the administration had ignored
the recommendations of a PACTS group in which the union had participated. The Union had a right to be concerned, but whether or not the
experience with PACTS called for a union boycott after less than eight
months is highly questionable.

Furthermore, the Board itself was reluctant to endorse the
PACTS concept. Indeed, in February 1975 the board indicated that it
might disband PACTS, and a story in the Washington Star-News referred to PACTS as a "controversial organization.[3] Board members have
said that the PACTS office has been used to organize citizens against
the board and to support the superintendent.

Two of the major forces, then, in Washington, D.C., school politics, the board and the union, have demonstrated open opposition to the
PACTS program. Added to this resistance is the style of the superintendent. Sizemore did not make any concerted effort to establish a
working relationship with the union upon taking office, and as indicated
in Chapter 3, the new superintendent and the board have been constantly
engaged in sparring tactics, almost since she accepted the position.

Summarizing, the failure to deal with the implications of PACTS
in negotiating the resistance by the board and the union, and the confrontation style of the superintendent, tend to illustrate the extreme
difficulty of altering the decision-making process in school systems,
particularly when those already holding some power perceive a new
organization to be a threat to their position.* This situation becomes
even more revealing when it is recalled that the union has been a bargaining agent for less than eight years, while the board has only been
an elected body since 1968. Both the union and those who ran for the
board in the late 1960s campaigned on some notion of increased participation in the schools by groups that had been consistently closed off

---

*PACTS has not totally failed. In October 1974 a PACTS worker
indicated that despite the union's official opposition to PACTS, a number of rank-and-file teachers had agreed to work with PACTS in their
respective schools. Overall, however, the program is struggling to
stay alive.

from the decision-making structure. Hence, neither had been in power
very long, and their rhetoric indicated support for concepts like community control. However, these groups, now that they could command
some authority, were more than reluctant to experiment, even on a
limited basis, with a concept that might have changed power relationships by introducing a new political institution. They were evidently
unable to struggle with the theoretical underpinnings of PACTS as expressed in this excerpt from its position paper:

> The terms negotiating and consensus are used because
> they come close to what we envision as the process
> used and the means of reaching agreement. In practice
> we hope to go beyond this.
>   If we move past being adversaries, PACTS will
> be exchanging ideas and views; being positively critical
> of the issues and the suggested approaches to issues;
> struggling with new forms of relationships and organi-
> zation. Essentially, what will happen is not a process
> whereby people compromise, but one in which a new
> idea will be developed from the different ideas that were
> originally submitted for negotiation. This new idea will
> include aspects of all of the ideas that warrant inclusion.
> This will perhaps be better described as "creative syn-
> thesis" than as negotiation and consensus.
>   As mentioned earlier, majority rule will have no
> place in this in that all components of PACTS must have
> their concerns represented and responded to. Students
> must represent students and be respected in that light.
> That they might be outnumbered by parents and teachers
> at a particular point should not negate their contributions,
> concerns and ability to influence the specifications to
> be decided upon.[4]

ADDITIONAL PROPOSALS
FOR REFORMING THE STRUCTURE

Responsive Board and Union

In its Report The Community at the Bargaining Table, the Institute for Responsive Education (IRE) study team identified a responsive
board as one means of opening up the bargaining structure, as follows:

> To make this approach viable, a board must view the
> community as its constituency in the same way the

leadership of a teachers' organization sees the teachers
as its constituency. A "responsive board" will develop
effective methods of communication and feedback from
the diverse parts of the community, including the "unor-
ganized" people who do not have representatives presenting their views and protecting their interests.[5]

Aside from electoral reforms or the training of school board
members, there are any number of methods for a board that decides
to include community views in the bargaining process. Already a few
boards are taking steps that hold promise, including, for example,
open hearings held before the formal negotiations begin and at intervals
during the process; inexpensive small sample sureveys such as that
which the League of Women Voters of Massachusetts conducted in the
spring of 1975; and the creation of school councils, similar to the
PACTS concept.*

Other possible techniques could be tried. The former president
of the Seattle Board of Education, who is currently the director of the
National Center for Dispute Settlement of the American Arbitration
Association, Alfred E. Cowles, has suggested that urban centers be
divided into subdistricts, from which parents would be elected to serve
on advisory negotiation councils. The board of education's negotiating
team would be obligated to have its demands approved by these citizen
councils. Under Cowles's plan, both the union and the board would hold
public meetings to confer with citizens about negotiations before formal

---

*On the question of public hearings, Harry H. Wellington and
Ralph K. Winter, Jr., have urged that in the public sector such hearings be required during negotiations. This procedure would allow citizens who might be affected by the outcome of negotiations to influence
the bargaining positions of the two parties. See The Unions and the
Cities, (Washington, D.C.: The Brookings Institution, 1971), pp. 150-
51. In a related matter, a Florida Supreme Court has ruled that "meaningful collective bargaining in the circumstances here would be destroy-
ed if full publicity were accorded at each step of the negotiations." The
case came before the court when a citizen objected to private negotiating
sessions between the school board's negotiator and the union. In this
instance the citizen complaint was based on a Florida statute mandating
that all government bodies must hold public sessions where official action is taken. See Harry Edwards, "The Emerging Duty to Bargain in
the Public Sector," Michigan Law Review 71 (April 1973): 885-934. To
date, this case has not taken on national importance, but it does reveal
how courts might rule, based on labor law built up in the private sector
these last forty years.

bargaining was underway. He stressed, however, that only the board would have to submit its final package to the community.[6]

An organizer for the Michigan Federation of Teachers has proposed a plan similar to that of Cowles. He contends that both the union and the board should be placed in a position of explaining and defending their bargaining positions. Such exchange could result in either or both parties altering some of their demands, based on community input during the preparations of demands for negotiations.

It is to be noted that the IRE report does not call for a responsive union in the manner described here. The report's recommendations are confined only to the board. In the end, though, both the union and the board must be willing to make some sacrifices regarding the present process. The conclusion reached by the IRE with respect to board responsibility should also apply to the union. The IRE report states this as follows:

> For a "more responsive board" approach to be effective, board members would have to be willing to take a much more active role in decision-making than now seems to be the case. The board would also have to be willing to sacrifice some of the alleged efficiency and speed of the present highly-professionalized bilateral negotiations model, and to live with some of the untidyness [sic] and abrasiveness that is almost inevitable when decision-making becomes more open and participatory.[7]

Multilevel Bargaining

The multilevel bargaining* "model" is an adaptation of the common practice of supplementary contract negotiations in the private

------

*Multilevel bargaining is not to be confused with the concept of multilateral bargaining; the latter refers to a situation in which there are more than two groups involved in the bargaining process. For the most part, however, community groups operate outside the bargaining process. Kenneth McLennan and Michael H. Moskow have said that for this group to influence bargaining, it must be in a position "to impose a cost (economic, political or otherwise) on the parties to the agreement." In education, such groups operate to put pressure on either the union or board or both. In their study, McClennan and Moskow found that citizen groups concentrated all their attention on trying to influence the board rather than the union. In a multilateral situation, which many argue is the case in public-sector bargaining, it must be repeated that

sector. This is an approach commonly found in large decentralized industries and industrial unions (automobiles and steel, for example). A master contract is negotiated between management headquarters and the central negotiating team of the national or international union, and then supplementary contracts are negotiated by local management and local unions.*

---

citizen groups do not necessarily become directly involved in any aspect of negotiations. McClennan and Moskow's discussion of multilateral bargaining in education discloses the absence of community in participation in any critical decision-making role, although pressure-group tactics are not to be totally discounted. Moskow and McLennan wrote as follows:

> Theoretical considerations suggest the following: Interest group activity in public education is relatively high throughout the negotiation process in line with the multilateral characteristics of bargaining. There is an expected pause in activity during the hard bargaining stage while the interest groups observe the possible outcome and the school board addresses itself to the details of teacher demands. Prior to the strike deadline there is an upswing in activity in anticipation of the strike although the interest groups now shift their attention from the contents of the agreement to pressure on the parties to reach agreement without a work stoppage. This trend continues and even intensifies if schools are closed due to a strike. Eventually group pressure may level off as the community either adjusts to the work stoppage or because the community temporarily establishes school facilities perhaps with the community involved in teaching. Most evidence, however, suggests that the community cannot supply the staff to keep the school operating effectively for more than a week or so.

For a complete discussion of this concept, see Kenneth McClennan and Michael H. Moskow, "Public Education," in Emerging Sectors of Collective Bargaining, edited by Seymour L. Wolfbein (Braintree, Mass.: D. H. Mark Publishing, 1970), pp. 219-60. See also Thomas Kochan, "A Theory of Multilateral Collective Bargaining in City Government," Industrial and Labor Relations Review 27 (July 1974): 525-42.

*In 1969-70 the Washington Teachers Union and the Morgan Community School entered into discussions about the possibility of negotiating a supplementary agreement. Unfortunately, the election of several new board members and the sudden departure of over half the school's teaching staff, all of whom were union members, brought an end to the experiment.

Such an approach might be feasible in school districts that are decentralized either by district or by individual school. The "master contract" between the central board and the city-wide union would deal with basic economic issues and a few other city-wide policy questions, leaving many of the issues affecting specific areas of the city or individual schools to decentralized negotiations. This latter point cannot be emphasized enough. This factor was highlighted as follows in the New York City Bar Report,* the thrust of which is directly applicable to the concept of multilevel bargaining:

> One of the most important steps is the establishment of a framework and ground rules under which disagreements between the City Board and the community boards as to scope of bargaining can be resolved. Scope of bargaining—what the parties must, or will talk about—is of great importance to the community boards. If the Chancellor and the City Board take the position that they will negotiate on virtually any matter raised by the unions, even though they are not required by the Taylor Law to do so, then the possibility exists that centrally-negotiated agreements will so circumscribe the community boards' authority to operate the schools as to render that authority meaningless. The converse is also true. The narrower the range of issues on which the City Board and Chancellor will voluntarily bargain, the greater the possible impact of the community board on educational policies in the schools for which they are responsible. Thus, what the Chancellor and the City Board agree to talk about is a key issue to the community boards.[8]

Harry H. Wellington and Ralph K. Winter, Jr., have also proposed a plan that reflects a multilevel bargaining situation. Under their

---

*Interestingly, this report, while concerned with the rights of local boards in negotiations, still indicated its general acceptance of the existing process. "We are aware that collective bargaining is not a public process and that successful negotiations often depend on private discretion. And we do not . . . advocate public negotiations. All we are saying is that community board members of the bargaining team should not be required to operate without a full awareness of all the facts." The Association of the Bar of the City of New York, "The New York City School Decentralization Law and Its Effect on Collective Bargaining," report to the Association, New York, N.Y., May 1972.

suggestion, there would be two bargaining groups, one of which would bargain over the traditional subjects, namely salary, fringe benefits, and working conditions; this group would consist of the central board of education and the bargaining agent. The second group would be made up of the teacher organization, the board of education, and representatives elected by the community in a decentralized school district. Hence there would emerge a form of multilevel bargaining. With respect to the scope of negotiations, the local bargaining group would deal with all or some matters related to educational policy. As Wellington and Winter see it, "the three-party bargaining should aim for formal agreement which would be an accomodation of the interest groups primarily concerned, the teachers, school management, and the most affected patrons of a particular community."[9]

If one can draw any generalizations from a study done by McLennan and Moskow regarding teacher attitudes toward decentralization, this suggestion by Wellington and Winter might find a receptive audience among some teachers. McLennan and Moskow found that a majority of respondents in their survey were favorably disposed toward centralized negotiations for salary and fringe benefits and toward decentralized negotiations with respect to decisions concerning working conditions and the instructional program.[10] A large number favored negotiating at the school level when dealing with such items as teaching load, class size, and procedures for textbook selection.[11] However, it should be underscored that this study also revealed that teachers appear to believe that their own "professional competence is more important in decision making than is the viewpoint of the community, as presented by local board members."[12] It would appear that the teachers feel that the union can negotiate certain issues for them more successfully in a decentralized situation, yet it is of significance to note that the teachers believe they can gain more direct access to the decision-making process through negotiations at the school level. Importantly, the NEA and AFT research offices report that there are presently no multilevel teacher agreements.

The Ombudsman*

A new role of ombudsman could be created in school districts, with the sole task of participating in all major aspects of policy making, including the negotiating process. The ombudsman would be mandated

---

*This section, with the exception of the footnote, is the same as in the IRE Report.

to act as protector of the public interest, placing the highest priority
on the interests of students.

An office of ombudsman and the authority for it could be created
by state legislation or state department of education action and funded
from state sources, or the office could be created by local school-board
action and supported by school-district funds. The responsibilities of
the ombudsman would have to be carefully defined, with a minimum of
bureaucratic constraints and a clear mandate for continuous communication with all the groups and interests in the community. Existing
advisory groups, youth organizations, school councils, and citizens'
organizations could serve as channels of communication for the ombudsman, along with the other mechanisms that he or she creates.

This proposed role would differ from many ombudsman plans already in operation in that the ombudsman would not be asked to deal
with individual problems and grievances but would be an "independent
representative" of those groups now largely unrepresented in policy
making and collective bargaining.*

Limited Scope Bargaining

---

*The ombudsman idea also has been advanced as a way to protect
the rights of union members. J. H. Foegen, in "An Ombudsman as
Complement to the Grievance Procedure," Labor Law Journal 23 (May
1972): 293, has written:

> But unions also grow. First, because such a procedure
> has been negotiated does not mean that all employee
> gripes will be handled promptly. As organizations of
> any kind become larger a bureaucracy is created. Forms
> must be filled out, schedules met, briefs prepared, and
> meetings held. The resulting delay creates impatience
> with and mistrust of, the system.

Although this does not directly address the question of staff dominance,
this question is raised by such an observation. It is noteworthy that
in the 1971 contract negotiations the Washington Teachers Union proposed an ombudsman to handle all grievances not resolved at the building level. The proposal was flatly rejected by the board negotiator,
since such an arrangement would have diminished the power of his office. More than that, however, was the fact that if the proposal had
been incorporated into the agreement, it would have been a step toward
altering the day-to-day relationship between the union and the board.
It could have conceivably have involved a citizens group, since the
union was prepared to accept a citizens review committee to act as ombudsman.

A number of people, mostly scholars and some labor relations experts, support the idea of sharply limiting the scope of bargaining, keeping as many educationally significant issues and questions off limits as possible. Such an approach would severely reduce opportunities for teachers to deal with the educational issues important to them, in which they have a legitimate stake. However, narrowing the areas of bargaining, it is argued, leaves large areas of policy open for significant community influence through mechanisms other than negotiations, such as individual school policy and advisory councils. Nevertheless, it is doubtful whether school boards or central administrations would move to provide greater community access following the closing of the doors to teachers.

Bargaining can be limited by amending existing state laws covering labor relations, in the schools specifically or for public employees in general, or by new legislation. As noted in Chapter 2, very few states have chosen to specifically restrict the scope of negotiations through state statutes. It is extremely doubtful whether efforts to legislatively circumscribe the scope can be characterized as a reform of the bargaining structure. Some of the approaches already mentioned are designed to include some form of community participation in bargaining. Advocates of a limited scope of bargaining, such as Wellington and Winter, are no doubt genuinely concerned about what they describe as the disproportionate political power gained by unions through collective bargaining.* But, as indicated elsewhere, it is the union

----

*In The Union and the Cities (Washington, D.C.: The Brookings Institution, 1971), Wellington and Winter have proposed that the states create a commission of disinterested citizens, holding appointment from the governor, who would have the authority to conduct public hearings in order to decide whether there should be an expansion of bargainable issues in various public sector areas. The commission's recommendation would be submitted to the legislature for action. It is questionable how to define a "disinterested" citizen, however. Given the trend in state legislation, it appears unlikely that state legislatures have any desire to enter the bargaining process, which is exactly what this proposal could eventually lead to. Nonetheless, under Wisconsin's revised Employment Relations Act, tentative agreements between unions and state agencies are to be submitted to a joint legislative committee, which conducts public hearings and then proceeds to either accept or reject the agreements. If the proposed agreement is rejected, the parties return to negotiations. There is no example, as far as I have been able to ascertain, of this kind of procedure having been mandated in teacher negotiations. Whether this approach will be adopted by other state legislatures on a broader basis is not clear.

staff, not the rank-and-file teacher, that necessarily secures a place of power in educational decision making. Furthermore, legislative restrictions on scope would in no way insure access to the making of school policy by minorities, the poor, and, importantly, the teachers.

Even though teacher bargaining is still relatively young, it is highly unlikely that written restrictions on scope would have much effect in actual practice. Those who want restrictions recognize the right of professionals, particularly teachers, to have a significant say in the "mission of work." Defining legislation that would respect the right of teachers to shape policy while at the same time limiting scope is seen as a difficult, if not impossible, undertaking, although of course it would not be impossible if the action taken were to deny collective bargaining rights. This is not the trend today. In the end the scope issue might be better resolved if some kind of common agreement were to be worked out in the course of the month-by-month, year-by-year process of discussion and negotiations at the local level. The assumption here is that some of the other reforms that are aimed at including the historically disenfranchised would take place in this bargaining process.

In summary, all these approaches acknowledge the legitimacy of collective bargaining as an essentially bilateral institution. The techniques suggested are mild reforms, in that they would keep intact the existing structure. Still, the approaches if implemented would open important parts of the bargaining process to community groups. Substantial decision making would not be gained, except perhaps in the multi-level situation. In fact, these reforms would probably not greatly weaken the powers of the new technocrats, although there might be some erosion of their authority. However, there is still another alternative that might be considered, which is a structure similar to the PACTS concept. Essentially this alternative explores the possibility of multi-party negotiation relationships that in effect would undermine the bilateral structure.

For another view on why scope should be legally limited in teacher negotiations, see Ophelia H. Zeff, "California's Alternative to Collective Bargaining for Teachers: The Winton Act, 1965-74 and Proposals for Change," Pacific Law Journal 5 (July 1974): pp. 698-722. Arvid Anderson has also advocated the enactment of state arbitration statutes, which would among other things restrict the scope of the negotiations that could be arbitrated. See "Public Employee Collective Bargaining: The Changing of the Establishment," address before the American Mining Congress, Denver, Colorado, September 30, 1970 (mimeographed).

Radicalizing Bargaining: A New Structure

Of all the approaches suggested, the one that aroused the greatest amount of concern and opposition from nearly everyone interviewed was the notion of formal multiparty bargaining.* In essence, the central concept of this approach is that the community is an independent "third force." There are wide variations possible within the multiparty framework. Community or parent representatives might participate in negotiations as mediators, helping each party see the other's point of view and helping to identify promising compromises. Again, community representatives might serve as "watchdogs," to keep both sides honest and to see that the interests of the children are properly considered in the deliberations. Such parent representatives might function as self-interested third parties in the bargaining process, with their own demands and with the right to approve any final agreement.†

Questions of who will represent the "third force" and how they will be selected become important when this model is considered. Some have proposed the organizing of a parents union. This has occurred in Philadelphia, and parents are beginning to organize one in Washington, D.C. Others have suggested a coalition of existing

---

*In discussing this concept, it is patently recognized that multilateral situations have always operated in the politics of education. Behind-the-scenes pressure and "silent negotiations" with the mayor's office, the city council, and the chamber of commerce have frequently entered the "politics of bargaining." Such third-party activity, nonetheless, operates at the fringe of the bargaining process, with most of the decisions still being made through the bilateral structure. Often, in fact, these outside forces only seek to intervene to "preserve the peace," rather than to deal with many of the substantive issues being negoitated. More importantly, these traditional third parties seldom represent the views of the poor and/or the minorities in urban centers.

†Myron Lieberman has pointed out that parent groups are not subject to strict legal bargaining statutes, as is the case with boards of education and teachers unions. He has also raised the question of the accountability of a third party. Lieberman is most reluctant to endorse third-party participation in bargaining, but he ends with this observation: "The point to bear in mind is the relationship between the scope of negotiations and adequate representation. The broader the scope, the greater the danger of inadequate representation." See "A New Look At the Scope of Negotiations," School Management, December 12, 1972, p. 8.

citywide and neighborhood organizations, to select representatives and provide a liaison with diverse constituencies. An additional possibility is using the chairpeople of school councils to select community representatives. The school councils themselves could provide grassroots consideration of the issues on the table. School councils exist in many large city school systems already, such as Chicago, Los Angeles, Atlanta, Louisville, and New Haven.

Resistance to this concept has come from all quarters, and not simply from the rising young teachers unions. Not surprisingly, the new professionals have contended that the introduction of this idea would undermine, if not destroy, collective bargaining as we now have come to accept it. Union staff members and board negotiators see it as both a threat to their newly-won power within the educational political structure, and they perceive the entrance of a "third force" as disrupting an essentially orderly process, except when a strike occurs. Many elected board members resist the notion, holding that they already adequately represent the community.

Third party neutrals not only support the collective bargaining model, but also contend that with their expertise they can play a critical role in ironing out some of the political dilemmas of bargaining in the public sector. To them, the bilateral structure is a proven success. Theodore Kheel, a nationally renowned arbiter and mediator, has expressed a view shared by a large number of third-party neutrals as follows:

> Even in government the most effective technique to produce acceptable terms to resolve disputes is voluntary agreement of the parties and the best system we have for producing agreements between groups is collective bargaining even though it involves conflict and the possibility of disruption. There is no alternative. [13]

Third party neutrals also maintain that the entrance of a "third force" would only invite chaos, since community groups lack the skills, knowledge, and time demanded by the existing bargaining structure. In short, the new professionals respond from the perception of what bargaining is rather than by seriously entertaining any notions of what it ought to be if the dispossessed public is to have a decisive say in the operations of social service institutions.

There is no doubt that the new professionals have a case; their concerns are absolutely legitimate, and any alteration in the structure will have to take into account many of these just criticisms. Introduction of a "third force" in a formalized way could lead to the demise of collective bargaining as it is practiced today; that is, multiparty negotiations do present a definite threat to the established structure. The

question is not whether change would occur, but whether it could be
beneficial or harmful. In the meantime, there are very few examples
of actual multiparty negotiations.*

Since I initially considered this idea, my views have developed.
Originally I perceived multiparty bargaining as a way of bringing urban
community groups, mainly poor and other third-world parents, to the
bargaining table. This early conception of the problem was similar
to that quoted here:

> The right of employees has been determined to be pro-
> tected by the Freedom of Speech and Assembly provi-
> sions of the First Amendment of the Federal Constitu-
> tion. . . .
> It is, therefore, essential that our imagination
> be directed to developing procedures which are consist-
> ent with collective bargaining in the human services
> industries and which admit groups other than the unions
> and government management into the decision-making
> process.[14]

---

*In 1974 the state of Washington attempted to pass a bill that
would have included students as a third party in higher-education bargaining, but the bill was defeated. In Massachusetts, student representatives at Fitchburg State, Salem State, and North Adams State colleges
have actually participated in the negotiating sessions between the faculty and the administration; this is the only case I have uncovered in
which a third party joined the bargaining deliberations. However, the
students had no authority to prevent the parties from reaching agreement. The union and the administration, though, reported that the students achieved considerable power at the bargaining table, since both
parties sought the students' support. In terms of the issues, the students were primarily concerned about the governance and evaluation
of faculty members. On other issues they frequently remained silent.
A brief report on this situation was written by Philip Semas, "Three
Mass. Colleges Allow Students to Participate in Faculty Bargaining,"
The Chronicle of Higher Education, October 29, 1973, pp. 1-2. Exper-
iments like this could have implications for public-school bargaining,
and such a development bears watching. To gain one student perspective on bargaining in higher education see Linda Bond, "Impact of Collective Bargaining on Students," in Lifelong Learners—A New Clientele
for Higher Education, edited by Dyckman W. Vermilye (Washington,
D.C.: Jossey-Bass Publishers, 1974).

Such a concept, while unquestionably modifying the closed bargaining institution, is still founded on a basic acceptance of the existing institutions within public education. Community inclusion would still center around an adversary relationship. A new group could conceivably join the new professionals, thus creating a situation in which the techno-structure might actually expand, instead of having its power and authority reduced. Reduction of two-party power alone is not the answer, since it would simply result in a redistribution of power within the failing norms of the system.

Like a number of others, I am persuaded that radical alterations will have to take place in society in general and public schools in particular before we will be successful in having masses of people control the institutions that shape our lives. This does not mean that the reforms alluded to earlier in this chapter should not be undertaken;* nor does it mean that some form of third party negotiations should not begin. However, efforts should be initiated that might lead to a structure similar to PACTS. This suggests a coalition of administrators, teachers, and community residents at the local level. It suggests further that there will probably be confrontation with the new and the old professionals in working toward a structure that will aim to take control over the governance of local schools. The risks for all concerned could be enormous; similarly the gains for all concerned could be quite great. People might recognize the simultaneous need to alter institutions and themselves.

With a successful community collective, over a period of time collective bargaining would wither away. For this to happen, however, a transformation within people and institutions will have to occur. Such a development is not about to happen soon, not unless it is made to happen. Teachers and the exploited urban dwellers can no longer

---

*Mario Fantini, in What's Best for the Children? Resolving the Power Struggle between Parents and Teachers (New York: Doubleday, Anchor Press, 1974), cites in his last chapter a number of developments pointing to possible cooperative efforts between parents and teachers in setting up "schools of choice." For a general critique of this aspect of Fantini's work see Nat Hentoff, "The Greening of the Schools," Social Policy, July-August 1974, pp. 60-63. One salient criticism of Fantini is that he tends to ignore the overall power structure that has emerged with the rise of bargaining. Hentoff, for instance, identifies two of these groups when he says on pp. 61-62, "Fantini not only does not even begin to explore realistically how the politics of teacher unionism is going to get in the way of his pipe dream, but he also envisions that somehow administrators too will present no insoluble problem if his various, assuredly reasonable designs for implementing schools of choice are followed."

simply rely on a "victim mentality." It is time for these groups to initiate change—reliance on the new professionals, on electoral politics,
or on new government programs has proven insufficient. This approach
can be perceived as a romantic notion of the politics of liberation. Nothing could be more self-defeating than to leap for joy at an idea that
includes tranforming institutions in order to provide the masses with
greater control over their lives. This concept of a transitional move
from collective bargaining to a less adversarial relationship will be one
in which all must struggle to create a new institution.* In this instance,
the experience of others in another situation who were going through a
dynamic and drastic change is well worth recalling with the following
extract:

> To practice self-and mutual criticism well one had to
> cultivate objectivity in several ways. First, one had to
> be willing to be objective about oneself. One had to be
> willing to seek out that kernel of truth in any criticism

---

*An appealing concept expressed by many, including Hy Kornbluh,
could certainly be promoted at the initial stage of multiparty discussions. He has suggested in "Bargaining the Goals of Education and
Teachers," Changing Education (American Federation of Teachers,
Fall 1973), pp. 22-25, that within the bilateral framework, certain educational policies should not be decided in a tension-filled atmosphere,
such as bargaining. "What is needed," he has stated, "is the ability to
bargain for adequate alternative structures with enough decision-making
power or influence to guarantee an effective voice in the final decision-
making process." To achieve this he urges that, through bargaining,
joint councils or committees be established having real power that is
specified in the contract. There is no reason why these joint councils
need to be limited to teachers and administrators: they should be open
to community representation. Further, such councils could be established at either a regional and/or a local school level. Already any
number of union contracts contain provisions calling for the establishment of joint committees. Most of these committees are limited to
professionals, although, as we have seen, the Newark contract has a
provision allowing community groups to serve on the joint committee
dealing with accountability. Incidently, joint committees, which often
go unnoticed, point up another means by which unions have secured
some access to policy making. A similar proposal has been discussed
by Shirley Jackson, "Shared Curriculum Decision Making and Professional Negotiations," (Washington, D.C.: National Education Association, ERIC, 083-731, April 1974). This same idea is found in Paul
Prasow, Scope of Bargaining in the Public Sector: Concepts and Problems, (Washington, D.C.: U.S. Department of Labor, 1972), p. 50.

regardless of the manner in which it was presented.
Second, one had to be objective about others; one had to
evaluate others from a principled point of view with
the object of helping them to overcome their faults and
work more effectively. One had to raise others up, not
knock them down. In practice these two considerations
meant that one had to pay great attention to one's own
motives and methods when criticizing others, while dis-
regarding in the main the motives and methods used by
others toward oneself.

Above and beyond this, one had to cultivate the
courage to voice sincerely-held opinions regardless of
the views held by others, while at the same time show-
ing a willingness to listen to others and to change one's
own opinion when honestly convinced of error. To bow
with the wind, to go along with the crowd was an irre-
sponsible attitude that could never lead to anything but
trouble. . . . The reverse of this, to be arrogant and
unbending, was just as bad.[15]

In short, examination of our own outlook and values must occur
in this new multiparty relationship. There must be an adaptation of
Fanshen to fit our circumstances.* I hold no illusions that truly
"collective" negotiations will be readily received. A move of this
nature will demand greater personal, social, and political responsibility from the participants. The resistance by those holding authoritative
positions within the present bargaining framework—including state labor

---

*Fanshen was a new word created during the Chinese Revolution.
It means "to turn the body" or "to turn over." In the introduction of
his book Fanshen, William Hinton describes the broad meaning of
fanshen:

It meant to throw off superstition and study science,
to abolish "word blindness" and learn to read, to cease
considering women as chattels and establish equality
between the sexes, to do away with appointed village
magistrates and replace them with elected councils. It
means to enter a new world. (p. vii)

Hinton's Fanshen is the study of how one Chinese village built a new
world. See William Hinton, Fanshen: A Documentary of Revolution in
a Chinese Village (New York: Vintage Books, 1966).

boards, the NEA/AFT, labor relations experts, boards of education, and arbitrators (AAA)—will be formidable; yet it may well be that nothing short of such a radical transformation will suffice if equity and unity are to be pursued.

NOTES

1. Seymour Sarason, Charles Cheng, and Don Davies, "The Community at the Bargaining Table," report to the Institute for Responsive Education, Boston, Mass., 1975, p. 12.

2. Charles W. Cheng, "The Scope of Teacher Negotiations in the Evolutionary Development of the Creative Bargaining Process (mimeographed, Harvard Graduate School of Education, 1974).

3. Diane Brockett, "Board Considers Ending Group Sizemore Created," Washington Star-News, February 7, 1975, p. B-1.

4. Kenneth Haskins, "PACTS Position Paper," a mimeographed working draft, Washington, D.C., Spring 1974, p. 10.

5. Seymour Sarason, Charles Cheng, and Don Davies, "The Community at the Bargaining Table," report to the Institute for Responsive Education, Boston, Mass., 1975, pp. 42-43.

6. Alfred E. Cowles, interview, May 30, 1974.

7. Sarason, op. cit., p. 43.

8. The Association of the Bar of the City of New York, "The New York City School Decentralization Law and Its Effect on Collective Bargaining," report to the Association, New York, N.Y., May 1972, p. 6.

9. Harry H. Wellington and Ralph K. Winter, Jr., "Structuring Collective Bargaining in Public Employment," Yale Law Journal 79 (April 1970): 869.

10. Michael H. Moskow and Kenneth McLennan, "Teacher Negotiations and School Decentralization," in Community Control of Schools, edited by Henry M. Levin (New York: Clarion, 1970), p. 202.

11. Ibid.

12. Ibid., p. 197.

13. Theodore W. Kheel, "Strikes and Public Employment," Michigan Law Review 67 (March 1969): 942.

14. Jerome Lefkowitz, "Unionism in the Human Services Industries," Albany Law Review 36 (1972): 603-631.

15. William Hinton, Fanshen: A Documentary of Revolution in a Chinese Village (New York: Vintage Books, 1966), p. 395.

Up to now most people have thought of politics as just a
clash between special class, regional and ethnic interests
for a bigger share of the pie. Radicals and liberals, white,
black, Chicano, etc. have been chiefly concerned with the
redistribution of goods. Now we must recognize that politics is not chiefly a question of redistribution. It is a question of, first, deciding what kind of society we want to
live in and, then, participating in the continuing political
struggles necessary to create and develop that kind of
society.*

The overriding focus of this discussion has been on the question
of altering the current collective bargaining structure in teacher negotiations in order to provide adequate community participation. The
main concern has been with large urban school systems, and the community generally has been defined as the poor and other third-world
groups residing in the inner city—groups that have historically been
denied access to decision making in this nation's political institutions.
This study has found that the scope of bargaining between teachers
unions and school systems has expanded into various policy areas,
giving the unions increased power in defining the public interest and
leaving these "disenfranchised" community groups even further away
from sufficient participation in the educational policy-making process.
A subordinate focus of this book has been on the ascendancy of
three new classes of professionals in public education. These consist

---

*James Boggs, "A New Philosophy for Our Contradictions," Oak-
land University, Speech, January 21, 1975 (mimeographed).

of board negotiators, union staff, and third-party neutrals. I have
pointed out that these groups are becoming a dominant force in school
politics. With the uneven development in teacher bargaining across
the country, it is somewhat difficult to predict exactly what the full impact of this group will be on the future of public education, but nonetheless the trend in the states that have developed more maturity in teacher bargaining reveals that these new professionals are becoming a
major influence.

Thus, at the same time that the number of educational policy issues that are subject to negotiations has expanded, the power to debate
and resolve these issues has increasingly shifted to a small number of
professionals, who are not necessarily accountable to the public itself.

SUMMARY

Chapter 1 deals with the rise of collective bargaining in public
education. It was pointed out that both the NEA and the AFT, the two
largest national teacher organizations in the 1960s, turned to the bargaining model of the private sector in order to improve the hours,
wages, and working conditions of teachers. Drives to organize and
collective bargaining campaigns were highly successful, particularly
in urban centers, and by the end of the 1960s, teachers unions had
emerged as a new political force in public education. This advent of
bargaining brought an end to the unilateral control over educational
policy-making supposedly exercised by local school boards. In the initial stages of bargaining, teachers unions tended to concentrate their
efforts on improving the economic status of teachers. As economic
gains were achieved and the political base of the union secured, the
unions began to push more fervently for an expansion of the scope of
bargainable issues. This pressing for a widening of scope explicitly
brought teachers unions into the arena of educational policy making.
Bargaining, then, posed a real challenge to the prevailing power relationships in the educational establishment, but as teachers unions began
to broaden their demands, questions began to arise about whether the
bilateral bargaining structure was the proper political place to resolve
matters that deal with far-ranging educational policies.

Chapter 2 dealt with the scope of the bargaining question, concen-
trating in particular on how a number of state legislatures, labor relations boards, and courts were coping with the rise of teacher negotiations, especially with respect to scope. With few exceptions, those
states having comprehensive bargaining statutes have not sought to
carefully delineate what scope should be through legislation. It is clear
that increasingly more states are enacting bargaining statutes for public
employees and that probably by 1980 all states will have some form of

bargaining law covering the public sector. A number of states appear
to be relying on the precedent set in the private sector with regard to
scope; that is, they have begun to employ a mandatory-permissive rule
over what shall and what may be deemed proper subjects for negotiation. New York State has taken the lead in using this guideline.

Next, state cases dealing with the issue of scope were reviewed.
In general one of the most telling points about these cases was the emphasis given to deciding the scope question on a case-by-case basis.
As will be recalled, when the two parties are unable to resolve the
matter at the bargaining table, these cases are decided by a state
labor relations board. The statutes establishing these labor relations
boards provide for appellate procedures to the labor board and after
that to appropriate judiciary bodies. Using the case-by-case approach
has tended to result in an expansion of scope.

Aside from these state rulings, scope has also been widened by
the parties during negotiations. Indeed, a number of comprehensive
studies were cited in Chapter 2 that highlighted the fact that teachers
unions were in the vanguard of the professional employees becoming
involved in the determination of policy issues. To consider the ways
in which teachers unions have widened the area of scope, Chapter 3
examined teacher agreements in four cities—New York, Detroit, Washington, and Newark. The analysis was primarily limited to educational
policy and to working-conditions, issues that have become the concern
of urban community groups. The contractual evidence disclosed that
teachers unions have made significant encroachments into a number of
policy areas; yet the contractual provisions do not reveal that teachers
unions, as some teachers union critics claim, are the controlling power
in urban school districts today. A report on a study of teachers agreements in New York and California that appeared in the Fordham Urban
Law Journal concluded that local boards still had final say in policy
matters.[1] Teacher power is real, however. Certain contract clauses,
for instance, demonstrate that substantive power has been won in various policy areas. These same clauses often imply a veto power, which
is equivalent to the ability to shape the formation of policies. Vetoing
an entire experiment as the teachers union succeeded in doing in the
Ocean Hill-Brownsville demonstration project, also indicates that contractual power is only one aspect of the bargaining relationship.

Still another significant aspect of the bargaining process is the
day-to-day relationship between the union and the central administration. This is one of the areas in which union staffs have ascended to a
powerful position. It is also one way in which community groups are
sealed off from any measure of influence in the operation of schools.
For example, some of the unions' strength comes from the contractual
provisions creating joint board-union committees, but as was noted in
the four contracts, the community is rarely included in any of these
joint board-union committees established under the agreements. Also,

although the joint committees are commonly referred to as union-board committees, the board is always represented by the administrative staff, while the union's committee is often dominated by its professional staff.

Following this contract analysis, the general commentary on the scope issue by a number of authoritative experts in the field was discussed. While conceding that scope poses some special problems in the field of education, most observers believe it will expand because of the difficulty in distinguishing between working conditions and educational policy. This becomes more complex because even the advocates of generally restricted scope in public-sector bargaining agree that teacher groups in particular should have a definite voice in the "mission" of the agency. A number of these observers, although they are genuinely concerned that teachers unions will gain undue influence in decision making at the expense of other community interest groups, still maintain that the bilateral structure is the best way to mediate the differences between public employees and the government. There is an apparent belief that a balance can be struck with the assistance of third-party neutrals.

Third-party neutrals perceive their role as one of partially representing the community's interest. From the review of state laws, the literature, and state cases, it became evident that this group is indeed emerging as a pivotal force in the entire bargaining relationship and particularly with respect to the scope of negotiations. This group, like the unions and the board negotiators, insists that the bilateral structure is the most feasible model and that it can best represent the interests of workers and the community. With their expertise, third-party neutrals can be instrumental in resolving conflicting interests between employees and employers, as well as between both of those parties and the community.

Having discussed union participation in policy-making and pointed out that scope was unquestionably expanding, I turned in Chapter 4 to the question of what roles urban boards of education play in representing diverse interests of the citys' population and in determining educational policy. If the boards are representative bodies, the argument is made, community groups really have no legitimate case to make that they are excluded from the negotiating process; yet there is almost universal agreement that urban boards grossly neglect the interests of blacks, the poor, and other minority groups. Not only has it been found that these boards are unrepresentative of vast numbers of citizens, but several studies indicate that the real locus of power is vested within the school administrations rather than with the boards of education.

During the 1960s, with the emergence of bargaining and the civil rights movement, the educational power structure came under attack. Educators also came under indictment from a number of leading social

scientists. The legitimacy of public education was being questioned,
and the superintendency was no longer a sacred institution free from
public criticisms. These challenges eroded the unquestioned authority
of the school bureaucracy. Bargaining, as indicated earlier, also
served to reduce the authority of the old professionals because it gave
rise to a new class within the school administration. The board of education and the superintendent turned over the authority to bargain to
consultant lawyers and/or created a professional negotiating office
within the school hierarchy. During negotiations, where many crucial
long-range decisions are often made, the chief negotiator in effect sup-
planted the superintendent as the principal decision maker for the
school administration. Bargaining had the effect of removing the board
of education further away from this prime area of decision making.
Hence, even if a board is a representative body, which is not the case
in most cities, in significant ways it is not an integral part of the bargaining structure.

After discussing the increasing importance of board negotiators,
Chapter 4 concluded with a description of the rising power of two additional groups of professionals, union staff and third-party neutrals.
Thus the chapter depicted the development of a new technostructure
made up of these three groups, which are in strategic positions in the
bargaining process. In closing, it was noted that urban teachers unions,
at the early organizing stages, had worked together with a number of
urban community groups that were equally dissatisfied with the school
administration. Both the unions and the community groups had at the
outset a common enemy, the school administration. However, once
the union was able to attain a degree of political clout within the educational establishment it had recently been fighting, a break occurred
with some of its former community allies. This cleavage between
teachers unions and community groups widened with the emergence
of the community control movement.

Chapter 5 concentrated on the concept of community control,
placing it in relationship to the drive for teacher collective bargaining.
Community control was characterized by at least two features that
aroused the concern of unions: (1) demands about the setting of local
school policies, including the hiring and discharging of teachers, and
(2) demands that all personnel be held accountable for student performance. Community control became a threat to the newly-won centralized
power of the union because the community might obtain a decision-
making voice in a decentralized school system. Increased pressure
on the part of the union to expand the scope of bargaining often focused
on areas in which the community wanted a say.

The major thrust of Chapter 5 was to underline the increasing
gap between urban community groups and teachers unions, especially
as the scope of bargaining expanded while community control was being
handed a series of setbacks around the country, with the opposition led

by the AFT. Thus these community groups, many of whom had been active in the civil rights movement, found themselves still excluded from
educational decision making, the difference now being that bargaining
created another impenetrable layer in the political power structure.
The central question then reemerged: is there a way for parent groups
to participate in educational decision making, or is collective bargaining incompatible with the needs and aspirations of third-world communities in urban cities?

Having indicated the unrepresentative character of urban boards
of education, and having demonstrated the emergence of three new professional groups holding major sway in the bargaining structure, in
Chapter 6 this study explored some possible alternatives designed to
alter the bargaining structure in an effort to include community participation.

First, a summary was given of some 30 interviews with practi-
tioners and close observers of teacher negotiations. Nearly all of those
interviewed agreed that community groups, specifically blacks, other
minorities, and the poor, had a right to influence educational policy.
Most further agreed that urban boards did not represent the interests
of these groups. There was almost unanimous expectation that the scope
of bargaining would continue to widen. The interviewees, however,
were divided about how to resolve the public-sector bargaining dilemma:
how do you balance the legitimate claims of both the employees and the
urban community groups? While most were sure that it was unsound
to directly include community groups in the bargaining process, nonetheless a number of examples of various forms of community participation were cited. These examples ranged from a separate contract
negotiated by the Newark Teachers Union with a parent group to public
bargaining sessions conducted in Chicago. Some of these illustrations
were viewed as positive steps in opening up the bargaining process to
the public.

Second, a number of alternatives for modifying or reforming the
bargaining structure were proposed. These reforms were discussed
and identified as follows: (1) a responsive union and board that call for
community input during the formation of bargaining demands; (2) multilevel bargaining in which supplementary agreements to the master contract are negotiated with regional and/or local school boards in a large
urban system; (3) an ombudsman specifically functioning only in school
matters, including negotiations; and (4) limitation of the scope of bargaining through the passage of state statutes, the assumption being
that parents will then be asked to participate in educational policy making. With the exception of the last proposal, all others were viewed as
promising approaches for breaking the secrecy and "closed society"
character of the present bargaining situation. However, it was suggested that these reforms would basically maintain both the existing
bilateral structure of negotiations and the hierarchical order of the

school system. Again, these modifications would, in the main, preserve the newly-won power and status of the technostructure.

The fifth proposal called for multiparty negotiations. At the beginning the notion of a third party was conceived simply as a direct
approach to formally including community participants in the bargaining structure. Some who advocate this approach perceive multiparty
negotiations in this light; that is, another group joins the existing structure. This, of course, is what caused the greatest alarm among those
interviewed, since introduction of a "third force" at the table would be
inefficient and unstabilizing. Multiparty negotiations was universally
rejected as an alternative.

Given the resistance by the technostructure to multiparty bargaining, it appears likely that its main chance of developing in teacher negotiations could come only through state legislation. At present the state
statutes clearly divide the bargaining parties into two groups: employees and management. Without a statute mandating formal multiparty
participation, community involvement can only materialize where the
employer and employee mutually agree to include a third force, as was
the case in one Massachusetts state college situation. If tried, multiparty bargaining would represent the most direct access to the whole
bargaining process by community groups.

As was indicated, I have to a degree come to question my original
notions about multiparty bargaining. This concept is based on the premise that classroom teachers and the community they serve have to work
together in setting school policies. Nevertheless, multiparty bargaining would probably result in simply adding on to the present structure,
and what is equally important, the cornerstone of the relationship between teachers and parents would remain an adversary one. Instead
it has been suggested that the basic premise of collective bargaining
and its acceptance of the general political order should be seriously
challenged. This means, in this instance, that those who are interested
in changing urban schools must begin to probe the possibility of creating new political relationships and institutions that will indeed, over
a period of time, cause the withering away of collective bargaining. As
suggested, this development will not occur out of wishful thinking: it
must be made to happen. Only by intense political struggle can community and teachers bring such new "collective" relationships into being.
Altering the bargaining structure in and of itself is seen as being inadequate. Concomitant with institutional change must come a transformation in the social and political behavior of people.

THE FUTURE OF TEACHER BARGAINING

Although it appears that collective bargaining laws will develop on
a state-by-state basis, it will be recalled that in 1975 there were two

bills before Congress calling for a federal law guaranteeing collective
bargaining rights to public employees. The creation of a Public Employee Department within the AFL–CIO in 1974 may result in stronger
lobbying pressure for passage of a federal law, and given the liberal
leanings of the new Congress, federal legislation may be enacted by
1977. The implications that a federal statute might have for community participation in the bargaining process are unclear. Would it be
flexible enough to allow the states to modify the law to include community participation? Would a federal statute make it more difficult to
alter the bargaining structure?

Another significant development that is directly related to the
growth of collective bargaining is the possible merging of the two
largest teacher organizations in the country, the National Education
Association and the American Federation of Teachers. In 1974 the negotiations were broken off, but many observers believe that this is a
temporary state of affairs and that an eventual merger is probable.
The fact that NEA and AFT groups have already merged in New York
State is indicative of this development. Any merger of the two groups
holds enormous political implications: such a teachers organization
would be the largest single union in the United States. For our purposes,
however, the following relevant questions arise regarding the merger
issue. Would the new organization tend to stress professional autonomy,
thereby reducing the possibility of including parents in the decision-
making process? Would it be totally opposed to any approach that would
alter the collective bargaining structure? Would it look with disfavor
on any move to include parents in the bargaining process? Much though
these questions apply to these two organizations as they are now struc-
tured, they will become even more crucial in the event of a merger.

Two final points need to be made with respect to the growing
power of the unions. First, local unions, because of pressure from
the rank and file, must begin to question the hierarchies and the fundamental outlooks of their own organizations. Union members must begin
to examine the very structure and operations of their unions and then
formulate programs intended to alter the pervasive influence of union
staffs, wherever that influence opposes progressive educational reforms
and restricts rank-and-file participation in such reforms. Already the
evidence reveals that union staff members, as in the case with many
large industrial unions, will become the supreme decision makers.*

---

*The election of Arnold Miller to the presidency of the United
Mine Workers, by a grass-roots movement disenchanted with the union
bureaucracy then controlled by the incumbent, Tony Boyle, is a promising sign. A few months ago a rebel candidate in the largest regional
steel workers district in the country unseated the director, who was
backed by the president of the steel workers union, I. W. Abel. It is

Second, the difficulty in initiating proposals calling for change
in the mid-1970s stems from the real threat to job security within the
teaching profession. Teachers who are genuinely interested in opening
up the bargaining process to community groups or who wish to weaken
the union bureaucracy are now forced to turn to their "union bosses"
for job protection. Some recent statistics underline the reasons for
this concern. In its November 1974 issue the American Teacher reported 95,000 teachers unemployed for the 1974-75 school year, while
another 135,000 teachers have been forced to work in other fields.[2]
Asking unions to alter the bargaining structure is difficult in the best
of times, but asking for significant alterations in a poor economic
climate may be virtually impossible.

That there may be no misinterpretation of the above remarks, it
must be reiterated that teachers unions are not alone in seeking to preserve the status quo in bargaining. All the professionals cited in this
study tend to support the present structure. Therefore it is evident
that the community groups themselves will have to seek an alteration
in the bargaining process, since it is unlikely that any of the parties
now involved in the bargaining structure will come forward with a proposal to include them meaningfully in negotiations. The findings disclose that various community groups are concerned about this and are
interested in participating in some way in the collective-bargaining
process, but although there are growing signs of such community dissatisfaction with bargaining, there is not at present any national effort
on the part of parents, community advocate groups, or legislators to
seek a real alteration in the collective bargaining process.

A LINK IN THE STRUGGLE

---

too early to predict whether these isolated developments will lead to
wholesale revolt within organized labor; nor can one be certain that
these reform candidates will be successful in revamping their organizations to make them reflect worker control. By contrast, Albert Shanker, the president of the AFT and the AFT Executive Council, is cen-
tralizing power in traditional ways. In December 1974 Shanker and the
Council voted to set up a national loan assistance fund for all AFT state
affiliates, which are to use this money to hire organizers. There are
two important conditions attached to the loan: (1) all staff hired must
be approved by Shanker personally, and (2) the states must agree to
lend their organizers to the national staff for a period of up to twenty
days a year. It is readily apparent that actions such as this will increase staff control both on a state and a national level.

Efforts to reform urban public schools might not necessarily have any far-reaching implications for correcting inequities and injustices in the larger society. Urban schools, however, are one of the areas demanding vast changes. An attempt to include community participation in the bargaining process is only one of the courses of action needed to bring about other, larger-scale political and economic changes. Altering the bargaining process along the lines suggested might have several important effects. (1) It could weaken the dominant control of the educational technostructure. (2) It could provide black, poor, and minority parents and classroom teachers with increased local power, on the theory that those who will be affected by decisions should stand in a meaningful relationship to the decision-making process. (3) It could promote radical improvements in the instructional program. (4) It could build new relationships between parents and teachers that would enable them to forge a constructive alliance extending beyond immediate school concerns.

TWO PATHS

No struggle for political change is easy. Frederick Douglass stated it eloquently many years ago, as follows:

> If there is no struggle, there is no progress. Those who profess to favor freedom, and yet deprecate agitation are men who want crops without plowing up the ground. They want rain without thunder and lightning. They want the ocean without the awful roar of its many waters. This struggle may be a moral one; or it may be a physical one; or it may be both moral and physical; but it must be a struggle. Power concedes nothing without a demand. It never did and never will. . . . Men may not get all they pay for in this world; but they must certainly pay for all they get.[3]

Today in public education, one of the groups making up the new professionals, the teachers union, is at a crossroads. In one direction it can pursue a policy of gaining more benefits and more power within the existing political order, a road traveled by nearly all AFL-CIO-affiliated unions since the early 1950s. Specifically, the union can define its professionalism defensively, and it can continue to insist that the bilateral bargaining structure is the only way to resolve issues of concern to teachers and community groups. The latter stance not only thwarts community attempts to influence school policy but also reveals a basic acceptance of the school hierarchy and of the authoritarian character of school systems. Whether following this path means inevitable clashes between parents and teachers remains to be seen.

The other path offers more risks and is more challenging. It means moving beyond established procedures and practices and taking a humane new direction. It means accepting greater social responsibility and demonstrating a willingness to create new alliances and new relationships that are not founded on political opportunism or on adversary relationships with the community. It means a commitment to explore, through practice, ways to include community participation in bargaining. It means that rank-and-file union members must decide whether they want a "union boss" or an organization controlled by its members. It means asking whether obtaining "teacher power" is sufficient to the task of educating the poor and blacks and other minorities. It means thinking about a new vision of what the union ought to be and what the overall society ought to look like ten or twenty years from now.

Both paths are fraught with uncertainties. The one that is more appealing to those wishing to maintain existing structures and relationships it is the well-worn path. Surely there will be difficulties and political skirmishes along this path, but such activity will be fought within the "secure" context of the limited hopes that now prevail. The second path demands more social and political responsibility from the people—in this instance from rank-and-file teachers and community groups. Reliance on the union structure, the electoral structure, and the bargaining structure must be rethought. Professional and lay relationships must be reconsidered. The time for reexamination is now.

It is hoped that this discussion has served to at least open up a reexamination of one of these structures in public education: collective bargaining. Change must be approached in such a way that it builds upon the gains won by teachers. For teachers bargaining has been an advancement, but the old stage in development must give way to the new. A new phase in the evolution of teacher unionism is upon us. Let us hope that teachers can create an alliance with the poor and blacks and other minorities that will see bargaining take a forward step toward the creation of a new relationship—a phase in development beyond our social and political imagination.

NOTES

1. See "Teacher Collective Bargaining: Who Runs the Schools?" Fordham Urban Law Journal (1973-74): 505-60.
2. American Teacher 59 (November 1974): 1.
3. Quoted in Lerone Bennett, Jr., Before the Mayflower: A History of the Negro in America 1619-1964 (rev. ed., Baltimore: Pelican, 1966), p. 274.

LEAGUE OF WOMEN VOTERS OF MASSACHUSETTS
120 Boylston Street
Boston, Massachusetts 02116

SURVEY ON COLLECTIVE BARGAINING
IN LOCAL SCHOOL DISTRICTS

1. What is the total number of school committee members in your district? Are there teachers or other professional educators serving on the school committee in your district? How many?

2. How is collective bargaining conducted in your district? (closed session or open public session?)
   If not open public sessions, are the bargaining proposals available to the public during negotiations? If so, how?

   Does the school committee inform the public of their general goals before the negotiations begin? Do they make interim reports? Do they make public the terms of the contract after it is signed? If so, what methods of informing the public are used?

3. Do you think that the public should be involved in negotiations? If not, for what reasons? If so, how?

4. How many members of the school committee participate in negotiations? How are they chosen? How many members of the teachers' association or union participate in negotiations? How are they chosen?

5. Does the school district use the services of a professional negotiator? If so, for how long have they been employing a professional negotiator? How is this person paid? (salary, per diem, other). Does the teachers' association use the services of a professional negotiator? If so, for how long? How is this person paid?

6. How many bargaining units or groups are there in your educational system? Who is included in each? (teachers, principals, administrators, other school employees). How does this composition

(grouping of employees for bargaining purposes) work? Would you propose any changes? For what reasons?

Are there interlocking clauses in the contracts of school employees and other employees in your town and/or school district? If so, what are the interlocking provisions?

7. Is there an understanding (written or otherwise) between the school committee and the teachers' association or union about which issues are negotiable and which issues are to be reserved for policy (i.e. school committee decisions)?

8. Which of the following issues are included within the scope of bargaining in your district?
salaries___school hours___determining class size___
student discipline policies or practices___curriculum___
placement of handicapped children___evaluation of teacher performance___ selection of textbooks___tenure rules and regulations___

9. Does your school district have a policy manual? Is there anything in the policy manual that relates to collective bargaining? If so, what are the areas covered?

10. Specifically, how are the interests of students being represented at the bargaining tables?

11. What, in your opinion are the major problems or problem areas in negotiations? What do you see as solutions?

12. What is your opinion of the new state law covering public sector collective bargaining as it applies to education districts?

Position of person interviewed:
   School committee member___
   Superintendent___
   Teacher association or union representative___
Years in present position___

Date_____   League_____

Please return by February 15, 1975   _____
                                                        Interviewer

LEAGUE OF WOMEN VOTERS OF MASSACHUSETTS
120 Boylston Street
Boston, Massachusetts 02116

TO: Leagues Participating in Survey
FROM: Ann Baird and Elaine Kistiakowsky-Education Committee

January 1975

SURVEY ON COLLECTIVE BARGAINING IN
LOCAL SCHOOL DISTRICTS BY
MASSACHUSETTS LEAGUE OF WOMEN VOTERS

Survey results due in state LWV office-February 15, 1975

GENERAL REMARKS

Through the survey interviews you will gain important information about collective bargaining decisions and processes by which
those decisions are reached. Most of the people you interview will
probably be aware of the League's long standing interest in education
and the issues that are important in educational decision-making. Our
interest in conducting a survey on collective bargaining stems from
our desire to increase the information available both to the public and
to our local education establishments. While we would like you to
treat the information confidentially (i.e. do not discuss persons interviewed or their remarks to your local League or town), you can inform
those you interview that the interview results will be treated anony-
mously (the identity of school district or school district personnel participating in the survey will not be used) and that those participating in
the survey will be the first to get the results of the statewide survey.
We think the information will be useful to them as well as to local
Leagues and the general public.

SUGGESTIONS FOR CONDUCTING THE INTERVIEWS.

We suggest that you do the interviews in teams of two. One person can record the answers while the other conducts the interview, or
both may wish to participate in the questioning and both keep notes for
greater accuracy. Please record responses on a separate sheet of
paper. (We will be especially grateful for typed responses!)
Make notes on information that comes out in conversation that
may not be part of the questionnaire, and write them on a separate
sheet. The more you learn, the better.

Make an appointment in advance stating the purpose of the interview. Try to get at least 45 minutes to an hour with each person interviewed.

Do not leave the survey to be filled out by someone else. Do not assume that an interview with your superintendent will make an interview with school committee members unnecessary (or the reverse). Interview school committee members (at least two), the superintendent, and a member of the local teachers' association who is knowledgeable about bargaining. Because many of the questions are open-ended, you, the interviewer, are essential to successful responses.

Your approach to the person interviewed is important too. Be pleasant and positive! Remember, this is an information-gathering procedure, not a confrontation. While the information we are seeking is not non-public information, be sensitive to the real possibility that no one may have ever asked these questions before.

Good luck! We wish you good interviews! We are anxious for your results—by February 15, please.

AGREEMENT BETWEEN NEWARK TEACHERS UNION
AND EXPERIMENTAL PROGRAMS

The Board and the Union agree that successful educational programs depend upon many factors, among which is the very important
factor of parent, student and employee confidence morale. To improve education and morale, the Board and the Union agree that
change and experimentation are essential to any ongoing process.

The Board and the Union agree that the Experimental Program
at Sussex Avenue School shall not violate any terms or provisions of
the present Board-Union Agreement.

It is further agreed that all rights, benefits and privileges shall
be maintained for the participating teachers during the length of the
program.

The Board and the Union agree to the following additional stipu-
lations:

A. All teachers in the program, including control teachers,
    shall be requested to attend one (1) week of workshops to be
    held during the regular school day.
       Full substitute coverage shall be provided for the partici-
    pating teacher.
       All teachers in the program, including control teachers,
    shall be entitled to the two preparation periods per week as
    agreed upon in the 1973-1976 Board-Union Agreement. Such
    preparation periods shall take place during the regular
    school day.
B. All teachers in the program, including control teachers,
    shall meet one (1) hour per week after regular school hours
    on a day to be mutually determined by parents and teachers.
       They shall be remunerated at the rate of ten ($10) dollars
    per hour.
C. In the event that teachers and parents mutually agree that
    additional days are required beyond the regular school cal-
    endar, the participating teachers shall be renumerated at
    fifty dollars ($50) per day.
D. The Board and the Union agree that the classroom teacher
    shall be considered the expert in curriculum, teaching meth-
    ods for this program. All evaluation procedures, materials

151

and questionnaires shall be jointly developed by the parents and teachers.

At the end of each six-week period, the Board and Union agree that teachers in the program shall meet with the Parents to evaluate this program. Any changes resulting from the re-evaluation shall be mutually agreed upon by the parents and teachers. These changes shall be implemented into the program at the beginning of the next six-week cycle.

E. Teachers shall not be required to sign any oaths, affirmations or endorsement letters concerning the Experimental Program.

F. The Board and the Union agree that nothing contained in this agreement shall be used as a precedent for introduction into any other school in Newark without negotiation and agreement between the parties.

G. Should any serious disagreement or conflict arise from this experimental project, the Union and the Board agree that the parents and the participating teachers will first meet to discuss the problem.

If the grievance is not satisfactorily resolved within five (5) school days, the teacher shall be allowed to withdraw from the program at the end of the first semester. Thirty days notice of withdrawal intentions shall be submitted in writing by the teacher to the Union and the Board.

The Board and Union agree that the teacher shall be returned to the same grade level previously assigned.

Agreement between the Board of Education of Taylor School District
and Taylor Federation of Teachers Local 1085 American Federation of Teachers AFL-CIO. Taylor, Mich. Effective September
28, 1973, through September 1, 1975.

Agreement between the Board of Education of the City of Newark and
the Newark Teachers Union, Local 481, American Federation
of Teachers, AFL-CIO. Newark, N.J. Effective February 1,
1973, through January 31, 1976.

Agreement between the Board of Education and the City School District
of New York and the United Federation of Teachers, Local 2,
American Federation of Teachers, AFL-CIO, Covering Day
School Classroom Teachers, etc. New York, N.Y. Effective
September 9, 1972, through September 9, 1975.

Agreement between the Board of Education of the District of Columbia
and the Washington Teachers Union. Washington, D.C. Effective
January 1969 through June 1971.

Agreement between the Board of Education of the District of Columbia
and the Washington Teachers Union. Washington, D.C. Effective June 1971 through March 1974.

Agreement between the Board of Education of the School District of the
City of Detroit and the Detroit Federation of Teachers, Local
231, American Federation of Teachers, AFL-CIO, Detroit,
Mich. Effective July 1, 1973, through July 1, 1974.

Agreement between the Board of School Trustees of the New Albany-
Floyd County Consolidated School Corporation and the New
Albany-Floyd County Education Association, 1974-1975. New
Albany, Ind. Effective 1974 through 1975.

Agreement between the Boston Teachers Union, Local 66, American
Federation of Teachers, AFL-CIO and the School Committee,
City of Boston. Boston, Mass. Effective September 1, 1973,
through August 31, 1974.

Agreement between the School District of the City of Highland Park
and the Highland Park Federation of Teachers, American Federation of Teachers, AFL-CIO. Highland Park, Mich. Effective
1972 through 1973.
153

Alutto, Joseph A., and Belasco, James A. "Determinants of Attitudi-
nal Militancy among Nurses and Teachers," Industrial and Labor
Relations Review 27 (January 1974): 216-27.

"An Act Relative to Collective Bargaining by Public Employees,"
S1929, The Commonwealth of Massachusetts, November 1975.

Anderson, Arvid. "Public Employee Collective Bargaining: TheChang-
ing of the Establishment." Mimeographed. Address before the
American Mining Congress, Denver, Colo., September 30, 1970.

____. "The Structure of Public Sector Bargaining." In Public Workers
and Public Unions, edited by Sam Zargonia, Englewood Cliffs,
N.J.: Prentice-Hall, 1972.

____. "School Policy and Collective Bargaining." Mimeographed. Mad-
ison: University of Wisconsin, 1973.

____. "The Impact of Public Sector Bargaining: An Essay Dedicated to
Nathan P. Fensinger," Reprint, Wisconsin Law Review, 1973,
pp. 986-1025.

Andree, Robert G. The Art of Negotiations. Lexington, Mass.: D. C.
Heath, 1971.

The Association of the Bar of the City of New York, The Committee on
Municipal Affairs and the Committee on Labor and Social Security Legislation. "The New York City School Decentralization Law
and Its Effect on Collective Bargaining." New York. May 1972.

Bard, Bernard. "Albert Shanker: A Portrait in Power," Phi Delta
Kappan, March 1975, pp. 466-72.

Bennett, Lerone, Jr. Before the Mayflower: A History of the Negro
in America 1619-1964. Rev. ed. Baltimore: Pelican, 1966.

Berube, Maurice R., and Gittell, Marilyn. Confrontation at Ocean
Hill-Brownsville. New York: Praeger Publishers, 1969.

Black Voters Rose Jolley et al. vs. John J. McDonough, Boston
School Committee et al. United States District Court for the
District of Massachusetts, March 1975.

Board of Higher Education of the City of New York and Professional
Staff Congress/CUNY. PERB Board Decisions. Albany, N.Y.:
State of New York Public Employment Relations Board, April 1974.

Boggs, Grace Lee. "The Search for Human Identity in America."
    Mimeographed. New Haven, Conn.: Yale University, 1974.

____. "Education: The Great Obsession." In "Education and Black
    Struggle: Notes from the Colonized World." Special Issue, Har-
    vard Educational Review, 1974, pp. 61-81.

Boggs, James, and Boggs, Grace Lee. Revolution and Evolution in
    the Twentieth Century. New York: Monthly Review Press, 1974.

Boggs, James. "A New Philosophy for our New Contradictions."
    Mimeographed. Rochester, Mich. New Charter College, Oak-
    land University, 1975.

Bok, Derek C., and Dunlop, John T. Labor and the American Com-
    munity. New York: Simon and Schuster, 1970.

Bond, Linda. "Impact of Collective Bargaining on Students." In Life-
    long Learners—A New Clientele for Higher Education, edited by
    Dyckman W. Vermilye, Washington, D.C.: Jossey-Bass Publish-
    ers, 1974.

Bornstein, Tim. "Federal Legislative Intervention in Public Sector
    Labor Relations for State and Local Governments." Mimeo-
    graphed. Washington, D.C.: Symposium on Equity and Public
    Employment, May 29, 1974.

Bowles, Samuel. "The Integration of Higher Education into the Wage
    Labor System." Mimeographed. Cambridge, Mass.: Harvard
    University, 1972.

Braun, Robert J. Teachers and Power: The Story of the American
    Federation of Teachers. New York: Simon and Schuster, 1972.

Brenton, Myron. What Happened to Teacher? New York: Avon Books,
    1970.

Brickhouse, George, Regional Director of the American Federation
    of Teachers, Washington, D.C. Interview, May 30, 1974.

Brockett, Diane. "Board Considers Ending Group Sizemore Created."
    Washington Star-News, February 7, 1975.

The Burden of Blame: A Report on the Ocean Hill-Brownsville School
    Controversy. New York: New York Civil Liberties Union, Octo-
    ber 1968.

Bussey, Ellen M. "Labor Relations in the Public Sector," Labor Law Journal 24 (August 1973): 512-16.

Carlton, Patrick W., and Goodwin, Harold I. The Collective Dilemma: Negotiations in Education. Worthington, Ohio: Charles Jones Publishing Co., 1969.

Carnoy, Martin. Education as Cultural Imperialism. New York: David McKay Co., 1974.

Chanin, Robert H. "Negotiations in Public Education: Developing a Legislative Framework." National Education Association, Washington, D. C.: ERIC Document Reproduction, Ed. 033 479, 1969.

Charters, W.W. "Social Class Analysis and the Control of Public Education," The Education Establishment, edited by Elizabeth L. and Michael Useem, Englewood Cliffs, N.J.: Prentice-Hall, 1974, pp. 98-113.

Chen, May Ying. "Lau vs Nichols: Landmark in Bilingual Education," Bridge, February 1975, pp. 3-7.

Cheng, Charles W. "The Scope of Teacher Negotiations in the Evolutionary Development of the Collective Bargaining Process." Mimeographed. Harvard Graduate School of Education, 1974.

City School District of the City of New Rochelle and New Rochelle Federation of Teachers, Local 280, AFT, AFL-CIO, Board Decision and Order. Albany, N.Y.: State of New York Public Employment Relations Board, July 1, 1971.

Clinton, Margaret, Graduate Assistant in Leadership of Educational Organizations at the University of Michigan. Ann Arbor, Mich. Interview, June 19, 1974.

Coleman, Herman, Executive Director of the Michigan Education Association, Cambridge, Mass. Interview, June 6, 1974.

Collective Bargaining in Public Employment and the Merit System. Washington, D.C.: U.S. Department of Labor, 1971.

Colosi, Tom, Assistant Director of the National Center for Dispute Settlement of the American Arbitration Association. Washington, D.C. Interview, May 30, 1974.

"Community Control and the Future of the AFT." A position paper by the New Caucus, American Federation of Teachers Annual Convention, Cleveland, Ohio, August 1968.

Corwin, Ronald G. Militant Professionalism: A Study of Organizational Conflict in High Schools. New York: Appleton-Century-Crofts, 1970.

Coulson, Robert. "The Public Employee and Arbitration," Journal of Collective Negotiations in the Public Sector 2 (Winter 1973): 5-12.

Cousins, Linda, Case Worker at the Massachusetts Advocacy Center, Boston, Mass. Interview, June 14, 1974.

Cowles, Alfred E., Director of The National Center for Dispute Settlement of the American Arbitration Association, Washington, D.C. Interview, May 30, 1974.

Crain, Robert L., and Street, David. "School Desegregation and School Decision Making." In The Politics of Urban Education, edited by Marilyn Gittell and Alan G. Hevesi. New York: Praeger Publishers, 1969.

Cronin, Joseph M. The Control of Urban Schools: Perspective on the Power of Educational Reformers. New York: The Free Press, 1973.

____. Secretary of Educational Affairs, Commonwealth of Massachusetts, Boston, Mass. Interview, September 10, 1974.

Dahl, Robert. Who Governs? New Haven, Conn.: Yale Paperbacks, 1961.

Dasher, Clare, Vice President of the Newark Teachers Union, Newark, N.J. Interview, June 18, 1974.

Davies, Don. "The Emerging Third Force in Education." Inequality in Education. Cambridge, Mass.: Center for Law and Education, Harvard University, 1973, pp. 3-17.

"Decentralization," District of Columbia Citizens for Better Public Education Bulletin Board, September 1974, pp. 1-2.

Derbabian, Arsh. Field Representative of the Michigan Federation of Teachers, Detroit, Mich. Interview, June 19, 1974.

Doherty, John, President of the Boston Teachers Union, Boston, Mass. Interview, June 13, 1974.

Doherty, Robert E., and Oberer, Walter E. Teachers, School Boards and Collective Bargaining: A Change of the Guard. Ithaca: New York State School of Industrial and Labor Relations, Cornell University, 1967.

Doherty, Robert E. "Public Employee Bargaining and the Conferral of Public Benefits," Labor Law Journal 22 (August 1971): 485-92.

_____. "Collective Negotiations and Policy Making in Public School Districts." Mimeographed. Institute of Management and Labor Relations, Rutgers University, 1972.

_____. "Public Bargaining and the Public Mood," Journal of Collective Negotiations in the Public Sector 2 (Winter 1973): 1-3.

_____. "The Politics of Public Sector Unionism," a review of The Union and the Cities by Harry Wellington and Ralph K. Winter, The Yale Law Journal 81 (March 1972): 758-71.

Duehay, Francis, City Council Member of the City of Cambridge, Cambridge, Mass. Interview, May 28, 1974.

Dunn, Frank, and Bailey, Thomas C. "Identifiable Trends in Teacher Attitudes Toward Collective Negotiation," Journal of Collective Negotiations in the Public Sector 2 (Spring 1973), 113-24.

Dupont, Ralph P., and Tobin, Robert D. "Teacher Negotiations into the Seventies," William and Mary Law Review 12 (Summer 1971): 711-49.

Dwyer, Jim, Member of the American Arbitration Association, Cambridge, Mass. Interview, June 6, 1974.

Edmonds, Ronald R. "Quality Education and Teacher Negotiations: A Non-Relationship." Mimeographed. First Annual Conference on Collective Negotiations in Education, University of Michigan, November 1972.

_____. "Minimum and Maximums: A Theory and Design of Social Service Reform." Mimeographed. Cambridge, Mass.: Center for Urban Studies, Harvard University, April 16, 1974.

____. "Advocating Inequity: A Critique of the Civil Rights Attorney in Class Action Desegregation Suits," The Black Law Journal 3 (1974): 176-83.

Edwards, Harry T. "The Emerging Duty to Bargain in the Public Sector," Michigan Law Review 71 (April 1973): 885-934.

Eliot, John, First Vice-President of the Detroit Federation of Teachers, Detroit, Mich. Interview, June 19, 1974.

Eliot, Thomas H. "Toward an Understanding of Public School Politics." In Governing Education: A Reader on Politics, Power, and Public School Policy, edited by Alan Rosenthal, New York: Doubleday, Anchor Press, 1969.

Elsila, David, Editor of American Teacher, Washington, D.C. Interviews, May 29, 1974, July 10, 1974, and January 5, 1975.

Elwell, John, secondary teacher in the District of Columbia Public School System. Washington, D.C. Interview, January 5, 1975.

Engel, Ross A. "Teacher Negotiation: History and Comment," Journal of Law and Education 1 (July 1972): 487-95.

Epstein, Benjamin. "What is Negotiable?", National Association of Secondary School Principals, National Education Association, Washington, D.C.: 1969.

Evers, Irving C. "Public Collective Negotiations—Some Problems," The Urban Lawyer 3 (Winter 1971): 337-43.

Fantini, Mario. "Community Participation." In The Politics of Urban Education, edited by Marilyn Gittell and Alan G. Hevesi. New York: Praeger Publishers, 1969.

____. What's Best for the Children? Resolving the Power Struggle between Parents and Teachers. New York: Doubleday, Anchor Press, 1974.

____. and Gittell, Marilyn. Decentralization: Achieving Reform. New York: Praeger Publishers, 1973.

Featherstone, Joseph. "Community Control of Our Schools," The New Republic, January 13, 1968, pp. 16-19.

_____. "A Failure of Political Imagination," a review of The Coming of Post-Industrial Society, by Daniel Bell, The New Republic, September 15, 1973, pp. 23-29.

_____."A Failure of Political Imagination II," a review of The Coming of Post-Industrial Society, by Daniel Bell, The New Republic, September 22, 1973, pp. 25-28.

_____."Youth Deferred," a review of Youth: Transition to Adulthood by James Coleman, The New Republic, August 24, 1974, pp. 23-27.

_____."Youth Deferred - II," a review of Youth: Transition to Adulthood by James Coleman, The New Republic, August 31, 1974, pp. 23-27.

Feely, Jeanette. "The Scope of Bargaining: Recent Effects of the Teacher Union Movement on Policy Matters in Public Education." Mimeographed. Amherst: University of Massachusetts, October 1973.

_____. secondary teacher in the District of Columbia Public Schools. Washington, D.C. Interview, January 5, 1975.

Fein, Leonard J. "Community Schools and Social Theory: The Limits of Universalism." In Community Control of Schools, edited by Henry M. Levin. New York: Clarion, 1970.

Fiske, Edward B. "Wealthy Districts Facing School Fiscal Challenge," New York Times, February 5, 1975, pp. C-35 and C-69.

Five State Organizing Committee for Community Control. "A Position Statement." Mimeographed. Cambridge, Mass., January 25, 1968.

Flynn, Ralph. Executive Director of the American Coalition of Public Employees. Washington, D.C. Interview, June 19, 1974.

_____. "We Need a Wagner Act for Public Employees," Reprint, Washington Star-News, July 21, 1974.

Foegen, J. H. "An Ombudsman as Complement to the Grievance Procedure," Labor Law Journal 23 (May 1972): 289-94.

Foster, Badi G. "Democracy and Change: The Performance of School Board Members as Educational Innovators," Mimeographed. Harvard University, 1974.

Freire, Paulo. Pedagogy of the Oppressed. New York: Herder and Herder, 1972.

Friedman, Jane. "Union Chief Flays 'Attack' on Teachers," Boston Globe, December 8, 1974, p. A-20.

Galbraith, John Kenneth. Economics and the Public Purpose. Boston: Houghton Mifflin, 1973.

Gaskins, Al. Coordinator of Parents, Administrators, Community, Teachers, Students (PACTS), Washington, D.C. Interviews, April 4, 1974, October 3, 1974.

Gilman, Glen. "The Rochester School Crisis: A Report on the Use of Mediation in a Multi-Party Community Dispute." Mimeographed. Washington, D.C.: The National Center for Dispute Settlement, May 1972.

Gintis, Herbert. "Alienation in Capitalist Society." In The Capitalist System, edited by Richard C. Edwards, Michael Reich, and Thomas E. Weisskopf. Englewood Cliffs, N.J.: Prentice-Hall, 1972.

Gittell, Marilyn, and Hevesi, Alan G., eds. The Politics of Urban Education. New York: Praeger Publishers, 1969.

____. "The Balance of Power and the Community School." In Community Control of Schools, edited by Henry M. Levin. New York: Clarion, 1970.

Golightly, Cornelius. President of the Detroit Board of Education, Detroit, Mich. Interview, June 20, 1970.

Government Employee Relations Report. Washington, D.C.: Bureau of National Affairs, July 1, 1974.

____. Washington, D.C.: Bureau of National Affairs, July 8, 1974.

____. Washington, D.C.: Bureau of National Affairs, November 11, 1974.

____. Washington, D.C.: Bureau of National Affairs, November 25, 1974.

Greenbaum, William N., and Cronin, Joseph M. "School Board Decision-Making: The Education of Children and the Employment of Adults." Mimeographed. Cambridge, Mass.: Harvard University, 1971.

Hamilton, Charles V. "Race and Education: A Search for Legitimacy,"
    Reprint Series No. 3, Harvard Educational Review, 1969, pp.
    47-62.

_____ and Carmichael, Stokely. Black Power and the Politics of Liber-
    ation in America. New York: Vintage, 1967.

Hanslowe, Kurt L., and Oberer, Walter E. "Determining the Scope of
    Negotiations under Public Employment Relations Statutes," Indus-
    trial and Labor Relations Review 24 (April 1971): 432-41.

Harrison, Nancy. Executive Director of D.C. Citizens for Better Pub-
    lic Education. Washington, D.C. Interview, June 18, 1974.

Haskins, Kenneth W. "The Case for Local Control," Saturday Review,
    January 11, 1969, pp. 52-54.

_____. "A Black Perspective on Community Control." Inequality in Edu-
    cation. Center for Law and Education, Harvard University, No-
    vember, 1973, pp. 23-34.

_____. Vice-superintendent District of Columbia Public Schools, Wash-
    ington, D.C. Interview, November 16, 1973.

_____. "PACTS Position Paper." District of Columbia Public Schools,
    mimeographed. Washington, D.C., Spring 1974.

Hazard, William R. "Collective Bargaining and School Governance,"
    Southwestern University Law Review 5 (Spring 1973): 83-117.

_____. "Courts in the Saddle: School Boards Out," Phi Delta Kappan,
    December 1974, pp. 259-61.

Helsby, Robert D. "A Political System for a Political World in Pub-
    lic Sector Labor Relations," Labor Law Journal 24 (August
    1973), 504-11.

_____. "Federal Law and Public Sector Bargaining." In "Symposium:
    Equity and Public Employment," Mimeographed. Washington,
    D.C., May 29, 1974.

Hentoff, Nat. "The Greening of the Schools," a review of Schools of
    Choice by Mario Fantini. Social Policy, July-August 1974, pp.
    60-63.

Herndon, Terry. "The Future of Negotiations for Teachers." In The Collective Dilemma: Negotiations in Education, edited by Patrick W. Carlton and Harold I. Goodwin. Worthington, Ohio: Charles Jones Publishing Co., 1969.

"Hugh Scott Says." District of Columbia Citizens for Better Public Education Bulletin Board, December 1974, pp. 1, 2, 5.

Immerman, Rita J. "Administrative Attitudes toward Labor Conflict Resolution in the Public Sector: An Empirical Investigation," Journal of Collective Negotiations 2 (Winter 1973): 97-112.

Jackson, Shirley. "Shared Curriculum Decision Making and Professional Negotiations." National Education Association, Bethesda, Md.: ERIC Document Reproduction Service, ED 083 731, April 1974.

Jencks, Christopher. "Who Should Control Education?" In Foundations of Education: Dissenting Views, edited by James J. Shields and Colin Greer. New York: John Wiley and Sons, 1974.

Jones, David R. "Militancy Sweeping U.S. Schools as Dissatisfied Teachers Turn to Strikes," New York Times, June 21, 1967, p. 85.

Jones, Leslie. Special Assistant for Labor Relations to the Mayor of the District of Columbia. Washington, D.C. Interview, October 4, 1974.

Jones, Ralph. Political Scientist at Harvard University, Cambridge, Mass. Interview, May 26, 1974.

Katz, Michael B. Class, Bureaucracy, and Schools: The Illusion of Educational Change in America. New York: Praeger Publishers, 1971.

Kheel, Theodore W. "Strikes and Public Employment," Michigan Law Review 67 (March 1969): 931-42.

____. "Collective Bargaining and Public Disputes," Reprint, Monthly Labor Review, January 1969.

Kilberg, William J. "Appropriate Subjects for Bargaining in Local Government Relations," Maryland Law Review 30 (Summer 1970): 179-98.

Kimbrough, Ralf D., and Williams, James O. "An Analysis of Power
    Bases and Power Uses in Teacher Militancy," In The Collective
    Dilemma: Negotiations in Education, edited by Patrick W. Carlton
    and Harold I. Goodwin. Worthington, Ohio: Charles Jones Pub-
    lishing, 1969.

Kirp, David L. "Collective Bargaining in Education: Professionals as
    a Political Interest Group," Journal of Public Law 21 (1972):
    323-38.

Klaus, Ida. "The Evolution of a Collective Bargaining Relationship in
    Public Education: New York City's Changing Seven-Year His-
    tory," Michigan Law Review 67 (March 1969): 1033-66.

Kochan, Thomas. "A Theory of Multilateral Collective Bargaining in
    City Government," Industrial and Labor Relations Review 27
    (July 1974): 525-42.

Koerner, James D. Who Controls American Education? Boston: Bea-
    con Press, 1968.

Kornbluh, Hy. "Bargaining the Goals of Education and Teachers,"
    Changing Education (American Federation of Teachers), Fall
    1973, pp. 22-25.

Kruger, Daniel H., and Schmidt, Charles T., Jr. Collective Bargain-
    ing in the Public Service. New York: Random House, 1969.

Leddy, John H. "Negotiating with School Teachers: Anatomy of a Mud-
    dle," Ohio State Law Journal 33 (1972): 811-29.

Lee, Robbie. Parent. Newark, N.J. Interview, June 18, 1974.

Lefkowitz, Jerome. "Unionism in the Human Services Industries,"
    Albany Law Review 36 (1972): 603-631.

____. Letter to author, November 12, 1974.

Levin, Henry M., ed. Community Control of Schools. New York:
    Clarion, 1970.

Lewellen, James R., and Sturbaum, Wilbert. "Power and Conflict in
    Educational Negotiations," Journal of Collective Negotiations in
    the Public Sector 2 (Spring 1973): 135-46.

Lieberman, Myron. The Future of Public Education. Chicago: The
    University of Chicago Press, Phoenix Books, 1960.

_____ and Moskow, Michael H. Collective Negotiations for Teachers.
    Chicago: Rand McNally and Co., 1966.

_____. "The Union Merger Movement: Will 3,500,000 Teachers Put It
    All Together?" Saturday Review, June 24, 1972, pp. 50-55.

_____. "A New Look at the Scope of Negotiations," School Management,
    December 12, 1972, p. 8.

_____. "Negotiations: Past, Present, and Future," School Management,
    May 1973, pp. 14-19.

Livingston, Frederick R. "Collective Bargaining and the School
Board." In Public Workers and Public Unions, edited by Sam
    Zagoria, Englewood Cliffs, N.J.: Prentice-Hall, 1972.

Love, Thomas M. A Study of the Impact of Collective Negotiations by
    Teacher Participation in the Making and Review of School Poli-
    cies. Madison: University of Wisconsin, ERIC Reproduction Ser-
    vice, ED 032 290, January 1968.

Lyke, Robert F. "Representation and Urban School Boards," In Com-
    munity Control of Schools, edited by Henry M. Levin. New York:
    Clarion 1970.

McKenzie, John P. "School Aides Liable to Suit," The Washington
    Post, February 26, 1975, pp. A-1 and A-5.

McKenzie, Robert B. "The Productivity Problem and What Can Be
    Done About it in the Public Sector," Mimeographed. Ithaca: In-
    stitute of Public Employment, Cornell University, 1973.

McLennan, Kenneth, and Moskow, Michael H. "Public Education."
    In Emerging Sectors of Collective Bargaining, edited by Seymour
    L. Wolfbein. Braintree, Mass.: D. H. Mark Publishing Co.,
    1970.

Macy, John W., Jr. "The Role of Bargaining in the Public Service,"
    In Public Workers and Public Unions, edited by Sam Zagoria.
    Englewood Cliffs, N.J.: Prentice-Hall, 1972.

"Maine's Public Labor Law," Maine Law Review 24 (1972): 73-97.

Marshall, Patrice. Parent. Newark, N.J. Interview, June 18, 1974.

"Martha Swaim Says," District of Columbia Citizens for Better Public Education Bulletin Board, December 1974, pp. 1, 2, 5.

Martin, Roscoe C. Government and the Suburban School. Syracuse: Syracuse University Press, 1962.

"The Mason-Dixon Lines Moves to New York," I. F. Stone's Weekly, November 4, 1968, pp. 1-4.

Mathews, Jay. "Sizemore Silent on Setback," Washington Post, December 9, 1974, p. C-6.

Mathews, John. Education Reporter for the Washington Star-News. Washington, D.C. Interview, June 18, 1974.

____. "Some Disgruntled Parents Moving Toward Own Union Here." Washington Star-News, February 21, 1975, pp. D-1 and D-4.

Maynard, Robert C. "Black Nationalism and Community Schools." In Community Control of Schools, edited by Henry M. Levin. New York: Clarion, 1969.

"Mayor Washington and the Teacher Dispute," Editorial, Washington Post, February 26, 1975, p. A-18.

Miller, Charles. "What Is Negotiable?" Changing Education (American Federation of Teachers), Fall 1973, pp. 25-27.

Miller, Etta. "An Analysis of Two Teacher Union Contracts with Large Urban School Systems." New York: Center for Urban Education, ERIC Document Reproduction, ED 088-239, April 1969.

Moore, William J., and Marshall, Mary. "Growth of Teachers' Organization: A Conceptual Framework," Journal of Collective Negotiations in the Public Sector 2 (Summer 1973): 271-98.

Morgenthau, Hans J. "Decline of Democratic Government," The New Republic, November 9, 1974, pp. 13-18.

Moskow, Michael H. Teachers and Unions. Philadelphia: University of Pennsylvania Press, 1968.

_____ and McLennan, Kenneth. "Teacher Negotiations and School Decentralization." In Community Control of Schools, edited by
Henry M. Levin. New York: Clarion, 1970.

Mrs. Lloyd Herdle et al., West Irondequoit Board of Education and
West Irondequoit Teachers Association. Albany: State of New
York Public Employee Relations Board, 1971.

Myers, Donald. Teacher Power—Professionalization and Collective
Bargaining. Lexington, Mass.: Lexington Books, 1973.

National Committee for Support of Public Schools. Proceedings of the
Sixth Annual National Conference for Support of Public Schools.
Washington, D.C.: the Committee, 1969.

National Education Association. Record of Resolutions adopted at 1973
NEA Convention. Portland, Oreg.: the NEA, 1973.

_____. Negotiation Research Digest. Washington, D.C.: the NEA, 1974.

Netusil, Anton J., and Mallas, Kenneth. "State Legislation and Collective Negotiation," The Clearing House, May 1973, pp. 519-
23.

Newman, Tony. Assistant Director of Collective Bargaining Research,
National Education Association. Washington, D.C. Interview,
June 19, 1974.

"New Teacher Contract Under Negotiation," District of Columbia Citizens for Better Public Education Bulletin Board, March 1974,
p. 1.

Odewahn, Charles A. "The Mediator in the Public Sector," Labor
Law Journal 23 (October 1972): 643-48.

Ofari, Earl. "Marxism, Nationalism, and Black Liberation," Monthly Review, March 1971, pp. 18-33.

Oliver, John. "The American Worker: Once Again the Victim,"
American Teacher, November 1974, pp. 15 and 18.

_____, Director of Collective Bargaining Research of the American
Federation of Teachers. Washington, D.C. Interviews, May 30,
1974, October 4, 1974, and January 4, 1975.

_____. "The Shrinking Apple: Teachers' Real Income Drops Again."
       American Federation of Teachers Report. Washington, D.C.,
       April 1974.

Patterson, Rochelle. "Public Workers Bargaining Bill Awaits Signing,"
       Boston Globe, November 23, 1973, p. 3.

Pegnetter, Richard. "Multi-Unit Bargaining in the Federal Govern-
       ment." Reprint, Washington, D.C.: The Bureau of National Af-
       fairs, 1973.

PERB News, Annual Report Edition. Albany: New York State Public
       Employment Relations Board, 1973.

Perry, Charles R., and Wildman, Wesley A. The Impact of Negotia-
       tions in Public Education: The Evidence from the Schools.
       Worthington, Ohio: Charles A. Jones Publishing Co., 1970.

Peterson, Iver. "Jersey Education: $ + $ = Quality," The New York
       Times, February 5, 1975, p. C-35.

Ping, Charles J. "Unionization and Institutional Planning," Educa-
       tional Record, Spring 1973, pp. 100-06.

Piven, Frances Fox, and Cloward, A. Richard. Regulating the Poor.
       New York: Vintage, 1971.

Pois, Joseph. "The Board and the General Superintendent." In Govern-
       ing Education: A Reader on Politics, Power and Public School
       Policy, edited by Alan Rosenthal. Garden City, N.Y.: Doubleday,
       Anchor Press, 1969.

"Public Employees—Court Adds 'Public Interest' to the Criteria Used
       for Determining Appropriate Bargaining Units—State U. Profes-
       sional Association of New Jersey Department of Education,"
       Seton Hall Law Review 5 (Summer 1974): 937-57.

Prasow, Paul, Kleingartner, Archie, Kaye, Edna H., Block, Howard
       S., et al. Scope of Bargaining in the Public Sector: Concepts and
       Problems. Washington, D.C.: U.S. Department of Labor, 1972.

Prince, Richard E. "Mrs. Sizemore Loses Power," Washington Post,
       December 7, 1974, pp. A-1 and A-4.

____. "Schools Quarrel Ebbing: Mrs. Sizemore, Board Seek Compromise," Washington Post, December 13, 1974, pp. C-1 and C-3.

"Project: Collective Bargaining and Politics in Public Employment," UCLA Law Review 19 (1971-72): 887-1051.

Quester, George H. "The Politics of Public-Sector Labor Relations: Some Predictions." Ithaca: Institute of Public Employment, Cornell University, 1973.

Raffel, Jeffrey A. A review of The Neighborhood-Based Politics of Education by Harry C. Summerfield, Harvard Educational Review 42 (February 1972): 126-39.

Randles, Harry E. "Toward an Understanding of Negotiation in the Public Sector, Part 1," Journal of Collective Negotiations in the Public Sector 2 (Spring 1973): 201-230.

____. "Toward an Understanding of Negotiations in the Public Sector, Part II," Journal of Collective Negotiations in the Public Sector 2 (Summer 1973): 231-56.

Raskin, Marcus G. "Ersatz Democracy and the Real Thing," The New Republic, November 9, 1974, pp. 28-30.

Rehmus, Charles M. "Fact-Finding and the Public Interest." Ithaca: Institute of Public Employment, Cornell University, January 1974.

Reinhold, Robert. "States Shift from Property Tax in Bid to Equalize School Funds," New York Times, February 5, 1975, pp. C-35 and C-69.

Report of the National Advisory Commission on Civil Disorders. New York: Bantam Books, 1968.

Ridgley, Robert L. "Collective Bargaining and Community Involvement in Education: The Trouble with Negotiations." Mimeographed. Boston: League of Women Voters of Massachusetts, 1974.

Rocha, Joseph R. "Collective Bargaining, Trends in the Public Sector," Journal of Collective Negotiations in the Public Sector 2 (Winter 1973): 77-96.

Roderick, Roger P. A review of The Impact of Negotiations in Public Education: The Evidence from the Schools by Charles R. Perry and Wesley A. Wildman, Industrial and Labor Relations Review 24 (April 1971): 471-72.

Rogers, David. "Obstacles to School Desegregation in New York City: A Benchmark Case." In The Politics of Urban Education, edited by Marilyn Gittell and Alan G. Hevesi, New York: Praeger Publishers, 1969.

Rosenthal, Alan. Pedagogues and Power: Teacher Groups in School Politics. Syracuse: Syracuse University Press, 1969.

_____, ed. Governing Education: A Reader on Politics, Power and Public School Policy. Garden City, N. Y.: Doubleday, Anchor Press, 1969.

Rubinstein, Annette T., ed. Schools Against Children: The Case for Community Control. New York: Monthly Review Press, 1970.

Ryan, William. Blaming the Victim. New York: Vintage, 1971.

Sabghir, Irving H. The Scope of Bargaining in Public Sector Collective Bargaining. Albany: New York State Public Employment Relations Board, 1970.

Sacks, Seymour. City Schools/Suburban Schools: A History of Fiscal Conflict. Syracuse: Syracuse University Press, 1972.

Salisbury, Robert H. "Schools and Politics in the Big City," Harvard Educational Review 37 (Summer 1967): 408-24.

Sarason, Seymour; Cheng, Charles; and Davies, Don. "The Community at the Bargaining Table." Report to the Institute for Responsive Education, Boston, Mass., 1975.

Schmidman, John. "Collective Bargaining in Pennsylvania's Public Sector: The First Three Months," Labor Law Journal 24 (November 1973): 755-63.

Schmidt, Charles T., Jr.; Parker, Hyman; and Repas, Bob. A Guide to Collective Negotiations in Education. East Lansing, Mich.: The School of Labor and Industrial Relations, Michigan State University, 1967.

Schwebel, Milton. Who Can Be Educated? New York: Grove Press, 1968.

____. "Collective Negotiations and Educational Reform." Mimeograph-
ed. New Brunswick: Institute of Management and Labor Relations, Rutgers University, 1972.

Seeley, David S. "Decentralization and Elections," In Report Card.
New York: Public Education Association, 1973.

____. "The 1972 Teacher Contract Negotiations." Mimeographed. New
York: Public Education Association, 1972.

Seidman, Joel. "State Legislation on Collective Bargaining by Public
Employees," Labor Law Journal 22 (January 1971): 13-22.

Selden, David. "A Momentous Year Begins," American Teacher, October 1973, p. 4.

Semas, Philip W. "3 Mass. Colleges Allow Students to Participate in
Faculty Bargaining," The Chronicle of Higher Education, October 29, 1973, pp. 1-2.

Shanker, Albert. "The Future of Teacher Involvement in Educational
Decision Making," In The Collective Dilemma: Negotiations in
Education, edited by Patrick W. Carlton and Harold I. Goodwin.
Worthington, Ohio: Charles Jones Publishing Co., 1969.

Shaw, Lee C., and Clark, Theodore R., Jr. "The Practical Differences between Public and Private Sector Collective Bargaining,"
UCLA Law Review 19 (1971-72): 867-86.

Shields, James J. "A Postscript: Social Reform as Educational Pol-
icy," Foundations of Education: Dissenting Views, edited by
James J. Shields and Colin Greer. New York: John Wiley and
Sons, 1974.

Shils, Edward B., and Whittier, C. Taylor. Teachers, Administrators, and Collective Bargaining. New York: Thomas Y.
Crowell, 1968.

Shipley, Grant F. "Determining the Scope of Bargaining under the
Indiana Education Employment Relations Act," Indiana Law
Journal 49 (Spring 1974): 460-81.

Siegel, Abraham. Associate Dean and Mediator of the Sloan School,
Massachusetts Institute of Technology. Cambridge, Mass. Interview, June 17, 1974.

Siegel, Jay S., and Kainen, Burton. "Political Forces in Public Sector Collective Bargaining." Catholic University of America Law Review 21 (1971-72): 581-88.

Silver, R. Jeanne, and Rebell, Michael. Memorandum to David Seeley, Director, Public Education Association. Mimeographed. New York: New York Lawyers' Committee for Civil Rights Under Law, 1972.

Simon, Larry G. "The School Finance Decisions: Collective Bargaining and Future Finance Systems." Yale Law Journal 82 (January 1973): 409-60.

Simons, William. President of the Washington Teachers Union. Washington, D.C. Interview, November 16, 1973 and October 4, 1974.

Simpkins, Edward. Dean of the School of Education, Wayne State University. Detroit, Mich. Interview June 19, 1974.

Sizemore, Barbara. "Decentralization." Public Schools of the District of Columbia, August, 1974. (Mimeographed)

Smith, Russell A. "State and Local Advisory Reports on Public Employment Labor Legislation: A Comparative Analysis," Michigan Law Review 67 (March 1969): 891-930.

"Some Remarks on the Board-Union Contract," District of Columbia Citizens for Better Public Education Bulletin Board, February 1974.

Sperling, John G. "Collective Bargaining and the Teacher Learning Process," American Federation of Teachers Quest Paper No. 11, Washington, D.C., August 1970.

Spero, Sterling, and Capozzola, John M. The Urban Community and Its Unionized Bureaucracy: Pressure Politics in Local Government Labor Relations. New York: Dunellen Publishing, 1973.

_____. Interview on Meet the Press. Reprinted in American Teacher, September 1974.

_____. "Teacher Unionism: A Quiet Revolution," The New York Times, Week in Review, October 28, 1973, p. 9.

Spring, Joel H. Education and the Rise of the Corporate State. Boston:
    Beacon Press, 1972.

Stanley, David T. Managing Local Government Under Union Pressure.
    Washington, D.C.: The Brookings Institution, 1972.

"Statement of the Black Caucus." National Conference of the National
    Committee for Support of the Public Schools, March 19, 1968.

Stieber, Jack. Public Employee Unionism. Washington, D.C.: The
    Brookings Institution, 1973.

Stinnett, T. M. Turmoil in Teaching: A History of the Organizational
    Struggle for America's Teachers. New York: The Macmillan Co.,
    1968.

____; Kleinman, Jack H.; and Ware, Martha L. Professional Negoti-
    ations in Public Education. New York: The Macmillan Co., 1966.

Strickman, Leonard P. "Community Control: Some Constitutional and
    Political Reservations," Inequality in Education (Center for Law
    and Education, Harvard University), no. 15 (November 1973),
    pp. 35-38.

Summers, Clyde W. "Public Employee Bargaining: A Political Per-
    spective," Yale Law Journal 83 (May 1974): 1156-1200.

Surkin, Carol. "Report Blasts School Politics," Boston Globe, Feb-
    ruary 27, 1975, p. 27.

"Teacher Collective Bargaining—Who Runs the Schools?" Fordham Ur-
    ban Law Journal 2 (1973-74): 505-60.

"Teacher Evaluation Criteria in Negotiated Contracts," Negotiations
    Research Digest. Washington, D.C.: National Education Asso-
    ciation, 1972.

"Teachers Strike Back," American Teacher, November 1974, p. 17.

"Testimony by Amy Billingsley at School Board Meeting," Washington,
    D.C.: District of Columbia Citizens for Better Public Education
    Bulletin Board, March 28, 1974.

"Time for a Change," Washington, D.C. Teacher, January 1975, pp.
    1-3.

"Total Control by UFT," Reprint of New York Times editorial, July 3, 1972.

Urofsky, Melvin, ed. Why Teachers Strike: Teachers' Rights and Community Control. Garden City, N.Y.: Doubleday, Anchor Press, 1970.

U.S. Commission on Civil Rights. Report: Toward Quality Education for Mexican Americans, Vol. 6. Washington, D.C.: the Commission, 1974.

Van Dyne, Larry. "Community Control Issue in School Problems of Cities." Reprint, Boston Globe, November 17, 1968.

Vermilye, Dyckman W., ed. Lifelong Learners—A New Clientele for Higher Education. Washington, D.C.: Jossey-Bass Publishers, 1974.

Walker, Jack L. "A Critique of the Elitist Theory of Democracy." In The Politics of Urban Education, edited by Marilyn Gittell and Alan G. Hevesi, New York: Praeger Press, 1969.

Walton, Jeanne. Regional Training Specialist in Day Care and Child Development at the University of Maryland. Washington, D.C. Interview June 17, 1974.

Weber, Arnold R. "The Federal Dragon and the State Knights: The Role of Federal Law in Public Sector Bargaining." In "Symposium: Equity and Public Employment," Mimeographed. March 25, 1974.

Wellington, Harry H., and Winter, Ralph K., Jr. "The Limits of Collective Bargaining in Public Employment," Yale Law Journal 78 (June 1969): 1107-1127.

_____. "Structuring Collective Bargaining in Public Employment," Yale Law Journal 79 (April 1970): 805-870.

_____. The Unions and the Cities. Washington, D.C.: The Brookings Institution, 1971.

West Irondequoit Teachers Association et al. vs. Robert D. Helsby et al. PERB Court Decisions. Albany, N.Y.: New York State Public Employment Relations Board, July 1974.

Wilcox, Preston. "Education for Black Humanism." New York City:
    National Association for African American Education, 1969.

Wildman, Wesley A. "What's Negotiable?" In The Collective Dilemma:
    Negotiations in Education, edited by Patrick W. Carlton and
    Harold I. Goodwin. Worthington, Ohio: Charles Jones Publishing
    Co., 1969.

Wilklow, Leighton, and Versnick, Henry, "A Management Team: An
    Approach to Negotiations," The Clearing House, September
    1972, pp. 8-11.

Wolfbein, Seymour, ed. Emerging Sectors of Collective Bargaining.
    Braintree, Mass.: D. H. Mark Publishing, 1970.

Wollett, Donald H. "The Coming Revolution in Public School Manage-
    ment," Michigan Law Review 67 (March 1969): 1017-32.

____. "The Bargaining Process in the Public Sector: What Is Bargain-
    able?" Oregon Law Review 51 (Fall 1971): 177-90.

Woodworth, Robert T., and Peterson, Richard B., ed. Collective Ne-
    gotiations for Public and Professional Employees. Palo Alto,
    Calif.: Scott Foresman and Co., 1969.

Work in America. Cambridge: The MIT Press, 1973.

Worsham, James. "Cronin Leaving with Warning: Control School
    Building Growth," Boston Globe, December 11, 1974, p. 49.

Yorktown Faculty Association and Yorktown School District No. 2.
    Albany: State of New York Public Employment Relations Board,
    1974.

Zagoria, Sam, ed. Public Workers and Public Unions. Englewood
    Cliffs, N.J.: Prentice-Hall, 1972.

Zeigler, Harmon. The Political Life of American Teachers. Engle-
    wood Cliffs, N.J.: Prentice-Hall, Spectrum, 1967.

CHARLES W. CHENG, Research Associate at the Center for Urban Studies of the Harvard Graduate School of Education, is a leading authority on community participation in collective bargaining in public education.

Prior to his faculty position at Harvard he had worked for seven years as a negotiator and organizer in the teacher union movement. From 1967-1972, he was assistant to the president of the Washington Teachers' Union and before that spent two years as an organizer with the Michigan Federation of Teachers.

Dr. Cheng received his doctorate in education from the Harvard Graduate School of Education in June 1975.

AUTONOMY AT WORK: A Sociotechnical Analysis
                        Gerald I. Susman

BARGAINING FOR JUSTICE: Case Disposition and
Reform in the Criminal Courts
                        Suzann R. Thomas Buckle
                        Leonard B. Buckle

THE SCOPE OF BARGAINING IN PUBLIC EMPLOYMENT
                        Joan Weitzman

WORKER MILITANCY AND ITS CONSEQUENCES,
1965-75
                        Solomon Barkin